Great Trails for Family Hiking

The Chapel of the Transfiguration, near Menor's Ferry, with the snow-covered Tetons as a backdrop.

THE TETONS

Great Trails
for
Family Hiking

Jerry Painter

Drawings by Clairice Mechling

PRUETT PUBLISHING COMPANY
BOULDER, COLORADO

© 1995 by Jerry Painter

Printed in the United States
10 9 8 7 6 5 4 3 2 1

Library of Congress Cataloging-in-Publication data

Painter, Jerry.
    Great trails for family hiking : the Tetons / by Jerry Painter.
        p.   cm.
    Includes index.
    ISBN 0-87108-857-6 (pbk.)
    1. Hiking—Teton Range (Wyo. and Idaho)—Guide books. 2. Hiking—Wyoming—Jackson Hole Area—Guide books. 3. Family recreation—Teton Range (Wyo. and Idaho)—Guidebooks. 4. Family recreation—Wyoming—Jackson Hole Area—Guidebooks. 5. Teton Range (Wyo. and Idaho)—Guidebooks. 6. Jackson Hole Area (Wyo.)—Guidebooks.
    I. Title.
    GV199.42.T483P35   1995
    796.5'1'0978755—dc20   95-3519
                                                        CIP

Cover design by Kathy McAffrey
Book design by Jody Chapel, Cover to Cover Design

Contents

Short Hikes and Half-Day Hikes   71

All-Day and Overnight Hikes   121

Acknowledgments

This book would not have been possible without my wonderful hiking companions and editors: My wife, Julie, and my children Levi, Leah, Sarah, Naomi and Samuel. We had great fun. Also my black retriever, Mitch, who managed to sneak along on some of the hikes outside of the park boundaries. They were the inspiration behind the hikes. I would also like to thank Eddie Bowman for his invaluable direction and critiques, and Sharlene Milligan of the Grand Teton Natural History Association for her assistance. I also thank Monte LaOrange for his photographic assistance and Clairice Mechling for her top-notch pen-and-ink drawings. Thanks to Terry Jensen for his willingness to share some of his favorite Teton haunts.

Introduction

Ah, the Tetons! These gorgeous mountains jut out of a level valley and reach skyward for several thousand feet. Their rugged beauty is classic: they're every bit as spectacular as the Alps. And for many visitors to this part of Wyoming and Idaho, viewing the picture-postcard scene from the driver's seat is not enough. That's how I feel. I want to really drink in the surroundings, to take a hike.

For many people, the Tetons mean multiday treks high into the wilderness with nothing to eat but freeze-dried spaghetti and ramen noodles. The Tetons do offer trails leading deep into the backcountry, but many of these are not appropriate for families. As a good friend once told me: "I spent several days with my wife and young daughter backpacking to a beautiful mountain lake. We viewed Jackson Hole from the crest of the Tetons. We saw wonderful wildlife. But I've never been able to get them to go since." Why? Because, although this was a dream trip for Dad, his tenderfeet hikers became burned out after the second day on the trail. No matter how fantastic the next lake or vista was, the price in effort for them was too dear.

This book concentrates on trails that are geared for family trips and that will hold the interest of younger hikers. Each trail is more than just a hike in the woods or a climb up a few hills. Some of them offer expansive views from atop a high ridge, others are hikes to waterfalls or hot springs; some offer walks through historic sites, others to superior wildlife viewing areas; and still others are just plain fun—offering fishing or aerial tram rides. If you visit the Tetons more than a few times, you can use these hikes as building blocks. You will notice that all the easy hikes are in the front of the book. Save the tougher hikes in the back of the book for another day, when everyone is stronger and more experienced.

Another nice thing about the hikes in this book is that most are within an hour's drive of Jackson, Wyoming. If you're from a city and an hour's drive sounds like a lot, don't worry. Driving in the Teton area can be half the enjoyment of being there. These drives are wonderful trips through scenic ranchland, over mountain passes, and along picturesque river gorges. You'll often see deer, elk, moose, waterfowl, and other critters on your way to the trailhead. And, except for a few tight intersections in downtown Jackson, the roads are usually a breeze. Most of the surroundng towns don't even have stoplights. Only Jackson has more than a few thousand residents.

Each time we take our families into the backcountry we're hoping for a bit of magic to make the experience unforgettable, especially when we have our children along. That bit of magic may come in the form of wildlife: a deer twenty yards ahead, walking slowly across the trail; a friendly squirrel that flits back and forth almost within touching distance; a group of elk, too intent on munching grass to acknowledge your presence.

Sometimes the magic is more elemental, as in a thundering waterfall along the trail or a vast glacier on a hot July day. Often, the magic is activity-oriented. For instance, in watching an eight-year-old reel in a two-pound trout or huff and puff to the top of a steep ridge to find breathtaking views of the surrounding mountain ranges.

But none of these things are a sure bet for that magical factor. Various things can steal the magic: the fish won't bite, the wildlife all seems to be elsewhere, or storm clouds roll in just before a trip to a special viewpoint. However, if there is a list of places where magical experiences are almost a sure bet, then the Teton area has to be on it. Variety of landscape is one major reason. The area boasts several large lakes, deep mountain forests, vast scrubby plains, breathtaking mountain crags, year-round snowfields, and impressive rivers and streams. And don't forget the animals. If you spend more than a few days in the area, expect to see a healthy supply of deer, elk, moose, bison, and antelope. Keep your eyes open for eagles, osprey, swans, geese, pelicans, ducks, and songbirds around the wetlands. And watch for marmots, pikas, squirrels, muskrats, beavers, porcupine, and martens throughout the area. It is not unusual to see representatives of half the above on a single hike.

The purpose of this book is to guide families to trails and walks that are almost always sure bets. The trails in this book not only take you into the backcountry but also offer something extra. And it's that something extra that can keep children excited to be puffing up a steep trail. The challenge for parents is to help family members understand that the activity itself can be the reward, not necessarily the possible results of the activity. If you do see a moose along Moose Creek or spy a circling bald eagle, that's icing on the cake. But if you prepare everyone to have fun simply hiking in the outdoors, enjoyment will not be dependent on something fantastic happening on each outing.

Be warned—these are the kinds of trails that can hook your kids into a lifetime love affair with the backcountry. Fun trails such as these are also a great introduction to backcountry hiking in general.

The trumpeter swan, largest swan in North America, is also on the endangered species list. The Yellowstone-Teton area boasts one of the largest populations in the world of this rare bird.

3

In the Teton Outdoors: Hazards and Precautions

The Teton area is a wild place with immutable natural laws. Visitors who forget to bring their common sense usually pay a price. Most injuries—and the few deaths—that mar each season in the Tetons are the result of carelessness or unpreparedness. Take care to familiarize yourself and your family with the different kinds of potential danger the Tetons can present. Knowing what dangers you might encounter is the first step toward avoiding them. The following is a brief overview of some of the major hazards you may face while hiking in the Tetons, along with advice on precautions you can take against them.

Weather

Most of the serious injuries and deaths in the Teton backcountry are associated with climbing accidents. But the hazard that affects everyone is the weather. Mountain weather is a source of constant fascination because its changes can be amazingly fast and dramatic. On one spring family hike, we watched the weather change from fifty degrees and sunny to snow, to sunny, to hail, to sunny, to rain, to sleet, to sunny, and back to rain again. About every half-hour a new cloud would pass over and drop its version of the day's weather. We never knew what would come next. The kids enjoyed the hike because we were all dressed for success.

Be forewarned: When you hike in the high country, it can snow during any month of the year. What may be a harmless drizzle at the the trailhead may be a blizzard two hours later and fifteen hundred feet higher at the top of the canyon. Although hiking in a July snowstorm may sound exciting, remember that the weather changes things. That easy-to-follow trail may disappear in a whiteout. Those rocks and logs, streams and puddles that do not require a second thought on the hike up become nasty obstacles on the way down.

A very common danger related to the weather is hypothermia. Hypothermia occurs when core body temperature drops to levels below normal, causing the body to malfunction in different ways. If the condition lasts too long, it is deadly. Hypothermia is usually brought on by wet clothes, cool breezes, and an empty stomach. Learn to spot this deadly foe in the early stages—before it becomes life-threatening. Symptoms usually consist of uncontrolled shivering, a stumbling walk, slurred speech, confusion, and difficulty getting fingers to do simple tasks such as tying knots. Another bad thing about hypothermia is that it makes you susceptible to other dangers, such as falling or getting lost. On the positive side, hypothermia is easy to avoid. Proper clothing, plenty of liquids, high-energy foods, and brisk activity will keep body temperature normal. It is important to remember that children can chill quickly.

Another major weather danger is lightning. Afternoon thunderstorms are common during the summer months in the Tetons and the higher elevation seems to intensify them. As in most western states, the flow of weather moves from west to east; it's a good idea to keep an eye on the clouds headed your way. If you hear the crack of lightning nearby, or hear buzzing in the rocks, or if your hair stands on end, seek protection immediately on lower ground. If you duck under a tree to keep out of the rain, be certain the tree is shorter and lower in elevation than those around it. Don't stand under or near a lone tree in a meadow. The places to avoid are high, open, exposed slopes; hills, ridges, and peaks; isolated or unusually tall trees; lakes, meadows, or open flats. The safest places are in caves, canyon bottoms, and in the part of the forest with the shortest trees.

It is helpful to know how far away lightning is striking

A marmot checks out the hikers from the safety of these rocks along the Cascade Canyon Trail.

in order to seek shelter, if necessary. You can get an approximate distance by counting the seconds between a lightning strike and the accompanying boom: Every five seconds in time means a mile in distance. So if you count eight seconds, then the lightning strike is one and

Color can be misleading when distinguishing between black bears and grizzly bears, but only black bears climb trees.

a half miles away. But remember that mountain weather travels fast. A cloud one mile away may give you only ten minutes' warning before it is upon you. One comforting thought is that summer thunderstorms are usually short-lived.

One final weather-related hazard is the sun. After reading about all the nasty things that can happen when clouds roll in, you may count yourself lucky to be hiking on a sunny day, and rightly so. But never underestimate the burning power of the sun at high altitudes. Before you begin hiking, no matter what the temperature, coat yourself and your children with sunblock. Put a little extra on your lips, nose, and the tops of your ears. To protect your eyes, wear sunglasses or a wide-brimmed hat, or both.

Wildlife

For many people, the Tetons are a great place to enjoy wildlife viewing. This area boasts one of the largest elk populations in North America. It is also home to large populations of moose, deer, bison, antelope, black bears, beavers, waterfowl, eagles, and snakes. In the Tetons, conflicts between wild animals and people are few. As one Grand Teton park ranger put it, you are more safe out on the mountain trails than on the highways traveling through the park. Bears get most of the press, but bear-people encounters in the Tetons are rare. Confrontations are even more rare. Bears usually see or hear people long before people see them, and they vanish.

What About Bears?

The Teton Mountains and the surrounding valleys and ranges is bear country. With a few simple guidelines, humans and bears should get along fine. These guidelines exist for the safety of visitors and the preservation of bears.

The Tetons are black bear country. Grizzly bears are usually found north of Jackson Lake on both sides of the mountains. In the coming years, though, grizzly bears are expected to increase in number throughout the park. Most people come to the Tetons and never see bears. If you see a bear, count yourself among the lucky. It is a rare treat.

Probably the worst thing that happens in the relations between people and bears is that bears obtain human food. When bears get a taste of human food they want more, and this often results in aggressive behavior. Aggressive bears pose a threat to people and eventually are removed to another area or destroyed.

Bears obtain human food from careless campers and hikers. Never leave packs with food or coolers or food baskets unattended. Keep a completely clean camp. Never cook inside your tent. Store food properly by hanging it out of reach of bears, or use bearproof food-storage boxes and poles where provided.

One reason bears are not seen often in the backcountry is their keen sense of hearing. They will hear you coming down the trail; they hear your footsteps and chatter. When a bear hears a human, it usually will leave the area.

If it stays put, it is usually because it doesn't perceive a threat. It will continue about its business and ignore you.

What you don't want, though, is to surprise a bear at close quarters. If surprised, a bear can react aggressively. Be careful in dense brush, along noisy streams, or during a loud wind. Make a little extra noise to lessen the chance of a sudden encounter. Singing or clapping or shouting (not necessarily at your children) can be of help.

Perhaps the best safeguard against bear attacks is hiking in numbers. Three is good, four is better. There is strength in numbers. No documented attacks have been reported against four adults.

Yellowstone National Park backcountry rangers often use a pepper spray against aggressive bears. These small pressurized canisters ride in a holster on a belt and work on the same principle as does mace spray. The powerful pepper spray immobilizes the charging bear and gives it something to remember for future encounters with humans. Pepper spray is sold in many sporting goods stores. If you decide to try it, look for the spray in concentrations of ten percent or higher.

Firearms are not a good idea. Besides being illegal inside all national parks, a gun would probably just serve to anger a bear rather than prevent an attack.

If you do encounter a bear, do not run. Bears are very fast, and humans can't outrun them. And running can encourage a bear to attack. If you encounter a bear that doesn't notice you, leave the area. If you encounter a bear that does notice you, let it know what you are by speaking in low tones while slowly leaving the area. *Never* feed or approach a bear.

If a bear charges or approaches you, do not run. Bears often use "bluff" charges to scare people away. Stand still and wait for the bear to stop its charge. Then leave the area slowly. Do not drop your pack—it can provide you some protection. Climbing trees is not as easy as it sounds, nor is it necessarily helpful: black bears are excellent tree climbers, and grizzly bears have a long reach.

The old Boy Scout joke seems apt: How do you tell a black bear from a grizzly bear when you are up the tree looking down? Answer: If the bear climbs up the tree and eats you, it's a black bear. If the bear knocks down the tree and eats you, it's a grizzly. There are, of course, better ways to tell the two bears apart. Color is a poor indicator—both kinds of bears range in color from black to blond. Black bears have a straight face, no shoulder hump, and a rump higher than the shoulders when the bear is standing on all fours. Black bears weigh from two hundred to three hundred pounds and are 2.5 to 3 feet at the shoulders. Grizzly bears have a dished face, small ears, a large shoulder hump, and a rump lower than the shoulders when the bear is on all fours. Grizzlies weigh from three hundred to seven hundred pounds and are 3.5 feet at the shoulder.

Other Wildlife

If you visit the Tetons for any length of time you can expect to see other wildlife. Despite continual warnings from park rangers, visitors to the area often treat wildlife as though they were in a petting zoo. Reports of tourists injured while trying to pet bison or get "just a little closer" for that great shot of a moose are all too common. "Let's get closer, Daddy," should sound a warning.

As with many of the dangers we encounter, common sense tells us that a thousand-pound animal that can run fast enough to break residential speed limits should be given plenty of distance. And that's the key: distance. Each animal has its comfort zone. When we stay outside this comfort zone, animals will munch placidly on grass or twigs and pay onlookers little attention. But as soon as we step within that comfort zone the animal becomes fidgety, shy, or aggressive. The usual result of our invasion is that the animal leaves, but occasionally an animal will attack what it sees as a threat. This is especially so for animals with babies.

To avoid ninety-nine percent of the potential problems with wild animals, follow these simple rules:
- Use a telephoto lens or binoculars to see animals up close.

- Leave pets at home. Dogs are not allowed in the park backcountry.
- Never get within one hundred yards of a bison, bear, or moose.
- Give all animals, especially ones with young, plenty of space.
- Never try to feed animals.
- Remember that small animals bite, too.

Avoid Getting Lost

Entire books have been written on the subject of how not to get lost in the wilderness. Most of the hikes in this book will not take families far from civilization, but when you are several miles from the trailhead, a wrong turn can be a big problem if night is only a few hours away. A good rule of thumb is that, if your hike is longer than a half-day, go prepared with the proper gear for spending the night. This may mean an extra couple of chocolate bars and an emergency space blanket.

But, as with most wilderness worries, common sense and prevention will help you avoid problems. Here are a few tips:

- Always take a map and compass, and know how to use both. Stop to orient yourself every mile or so. Involve the kids in this exercise.
- Don't panic, whatever happens. Panic is contagious and will cause you to do foolish things and burn up needless energy. If you take a wrong turn and lose an hour on the wrong trail, so what? Develop the attitude that the best part of hiking is in the trip, and not in slavishly reaching planned destinations.
- Always take along a flashlight. If you should get held up by weather or miscalculations or an angry moose and find your family hiking in the dark, a flashlight will be a lifesaver. A headlamp is helpful because it will free up your hands to help others.
- Take along a watch. With a rough estimate of how fast you walk, a watch will help place you on the map.

- Don't walk in a daydream. Pay attention to your surroundings so that if you backtrack you'll recognize where you are.
- Keep younger children in sight at all times. Tell everyone to regroup at all trail junctions.
- Take along a repair/emergency kit (see page 19).
- Know how to keep warm with minimal gear: stay out of the wind, cover up with leaves or in holes, take matches for a campfire, drink plenty of water.
- Never eat wild plants unless you can positively identify them as safe.
- Make sure children and parents all carry a whistle.

Outfitting Your Tribe

One of the nice things about hiking is that it doesn't require lots of fancy equipment or years of "getting good at it." Basically, you're just walking—something most of us have been doing well since childhood.

But hiking in the mountains is not a trip to the beach. It requires a bit more preparation than a bottle of suntan lotion and a towel. But despite what recreation-gear manufacturers would have us believe, only a few items are really required gear in a hiker's day pack. Usually, the fewer items you stuff in your pack, the fewer rest stops you'll be forced into taking. This is especially true for youngsters. The rule of thumb in hiking is if you don't use it on every hike, don't pack it.

But because the Tetons are mountains, follow the Boy Scout motto: Be prepared. Forgetting to bring along the proper gear here can have painful, even serious consequences. The following lists of gear should be useful as reminders, but be aware they are only appropriate for trail hiking. If you plan on going backpacking or hiking off the trail or climbing mountains, the following suggestions are insufficient.

For information on backpacking gear, see page 183, So, You Want to Go Backpacking.

Gear Checklist for Family Day Hiking

• **Footwear.** The key word here is comfort, particularly where little feet are concerned. In most cases, all any hiker needs is a pair of good thick-soled running shoes. These are lightweight and feel good the moment they go on. Kids can often get by with a pair of tennies or high-tops. If possible, get running shoes with some grip to the soles, which will help prevent slipping. For kids, make sure the shoes fit properly. This will help prevent blisters.

If you have weak ankles, you may consider some of the new lightweight high-top hiking shoes. The tops should go over your ankles to give extra support.

Parents who will be carrying extra weight, such as a child carrier loaded with baby and accessories, may find a stout pair of hiking boots offer more support. But unless you hike every weekend, I recommend not buying boots that require a great deal of breaking in. Most feet will appreciate the comfort of the newer lightweight hiking boots made with a combination of leather and lighter synthetic materials.

• **Socks.** Never underestimate their value. Avoid cotton socks—they cause blisters. The best socks I've found are made of a combination of wool and synthetic materials, such as Orlon.

• **Pants.** As with shoes, comfort is the watchword. Sweatpants are hard to beat, and sweatpants with pockets are even better. On warm summer days, loose-fitting shorts are fine, but remember that eighty degrees at the trailhead may change to fifty degrees a few hours later and two thousand feet higher. Long pants protect legs from sunburn and scratchy things along the trail.

I avoid jeans. Jeans are heavy and can sometimes chafe in tender places on long hikes. And once denim gets wet, it won't dry on the trail.

Nylon or polyester pants are nice because they dry quickly after getting wet. If you wear light cotton pants, it's a good idea to bring along rain pants to keep dry when thunderclouds roll in.

• **Upper body.** Think in layers. T-shirts are great

for warm weather, but make sure everyone has a long-sleeve sweater or vest, a windbreaker, *and* an inexpensive rain poncho in his or her pack. Many people prefer rain jackets and pants for better protection against blustery thundershowers. If the weather is cool at the trailhead, you may want to go prepared with a coat instead of just a windbreaker. Lightweight but very warm fleece coats with high collars can't be beat.

• **Headgear.** I recommend a wide-brimmed hat to block the sun, *and* a pair of sunglasses. Beware of sunglasses that don't block ultraviolet rays. Because it's hard to find good sunglasses in kid sizes, make sure children have a wide-brimmed hat or ball cap and wear them, even on cloudy days—at high altitudes it doesn't take long for eyes to get burned. Pack a warm stocking hat for each person on cooler days. These hats should cover the ears.

• **Hands.** A pair of mittens or gloves can be a big help on chilly days or against mountaintop breezes.

• **Packs.** Each child should have his or her own day pack. A school book pack is just fine. If you haven't yet purchased packs, get the kind with padded backs, padded shoulder straps, waist belts, and lots of extra pockets. Packs with padded backs are more comfortable and do double duty as soft, warm seat cushions. Children feel more a part of the adventure if they carry at least some of their stuff and a small item or two that will be used by the entire family—even if it's only the bug repellent. Besides the extra sweater and rain poncho, children can carry a snack or lunch and small water bottle. If each child carries his own water bottle, it's easy for parents to keep track of who is drinking the proper amounts of water.

Packs for Mom and Dad and teens can be a bit larger to accommodate the extra items the family uses. Beware of using too big a pack for day hiking; sometimes the extra space invites you to fill it with needless items.

If you have a toddler or baby, you will want to use a child-carrier pack. I don't recommend carrying a child on your shoulders for more than a quarter-mile. Your child may love it, but your shoulder muscles will begin to complain. For serious hiking distances, rent or buy a child carrier. Make sure it has a wide, padded, waist belt. The waist belt allows you to carry most of the weight on your hips. It's also handy to get carriers with extra pouches for your gear and baby's necessities. The best carriers allow the child to sit high enough to see over the parent's shoulders. Children soon become bored and fidgety if all they get to see of the hike is Dad's sweaty shoulderblades.

Remember that children riding in child carriers are more susceptible to cold, because they are not doing any work. You may be sweating up a hill, but the child should be bundled against the chilly mountain air.

• **First-Aid Kit.** Always bring along a first-aid kit (see the list on page 18) and know basic first-aid skills.

• **Repair/emergency kit.** This is a good idea on hikes of more than a couple miles. (See the list on page 19.)

• **Insect Repellent.** Mosquito and black fly repellent is a must in early summer. If you don't want to use or carry bug repellent, a good alternative is netting that drapes over a hat.

• **Maps.** Don't forget to take along a good map of the area you're hiking, especially if the trail is more than a couple miles. Without a map, a few forks in the path can sometimes get you mixed up and feeling unsure of yourself. If you are going for a long day hike, I suggest you also take along a compass and know how to use it.

• **Camera.** By all means, bring along a camera and plenty of film. Don't just snap shots of the great scenery. For every photo of a beautiful mountain or alpine lake, take two shots of your family members. Years from now the pictures will remind them of the adventures.

• **Miscellaneous Items.** Other items, depending on your interests, you may want to pack include binoculars, books for identifying wildlife and plants, or fishing gear. Needless to say, bring lightweight, down-sized versions of this gear whenever possible.

- **Walking Sticks.** I find a walking stick very useful. My walking stick has saved me from many a stumble when I've been hiking on loose rock or snow and when I've had to cross streams.
  - **Whistles.** Some families like to pack whistles. A whistle can help parents and children find one another if they become separated. Whistles should be used *only* in serious situations if they are to be helpful.
  - **Ground Pads.** Another great piece of gear is the Ensolite pad. These closed-cell foam pads are very lightweight, but they earn their keep when it comes time to eat lunch by making the toughest pile of rocks or the chilliest glacier a comfy roost. The six-foot long pads usually have enough room for all the rumps in the family.

First-Aid and Emergency Repairs

The old rule of thumb about packing hiking gear you don't use doesn't apply to your first-aid kit. You never want to leave it behind, but you hope you'll never have to use it.

The following list details what I put into my first-aid kit. If you are just getting started compiling a first-aid kit, I suggest you get all of the things on this list and then add and subtract items according to your experience with your family.

It's also very important to become competent at first aid and to teach your children first-aid practices as they grow older. As parents, we usually think in terms of patching up children on our outings, but on one occasion, while hiking over lava flows, I stepped on a disguised hole and was glad my son had earned his first-aid merit badge in Boy Scouts. It was a deep crack in the lava flows that was covered with snow. Down I went, smacking my face on the sharp lava rock. Because it was a cool day, I had my hands in my pockets (my hands *should* have been in my warm gloves, which I left back in the car). My son did the patch-up work. "You look pretty bad, Dad," he said. I didn't feel so good, either. We used the snow that once hid the hole so well to numb the pain and stop the gushing blood. With two miles yet to hike, I had my son give me periodic checkups.

Make sure you personalize your first-aid kit according to your family's needs. For instance, some family members may need special medication—don't forget it.

First-Aid Kit Checklist

❏ Unbreakable mirror (Helpful in getting things out of your eyes or patching up your face.)
❏ Adhesive tape
❏ Adhesive bandage strips
❏ Knuckle bandages
❏ Butterfly bandages (Band-Aid brand is fine.)
❏ Moleskin (Indispensable for preventing and cushioning blisters on your feet.)
❏ Elastic bandage (of the kind used for sprains)
❏ Needle and thread
❏ Antibiotic ointment
❏ Aspirin or equivalent
❏ Emergency blanket (These are the lightweight plastic or foil variety.)
❏ Bee-sting medicine (if anyone in your family is allergic.)
❏ Loose change for phone calls
❏ Antacid tablets
❏ Cold tablets
❏ Gauze
❏ Small pair of scissors
❏ Tweezers
❏ Booklet on first-aid techniques
❏ Sting-relief ointment
❏ Moist sanitizing towelettes
❏ Safety pins
❏ Matches
❏ Plastic box or pouch to contain all of the above

Emergency/Repair Kit Checklist

Certain things happen on hikes that can be a real nuisance—a pack strap breaks, shoelaces break, pants rip out in the worst places, and buttons fly off. But with a small ditty bag or plastic box with a few essentials, you'll be ready to cope with almost anything fate tosses your way. As with a first-aid kit, these repair-kit items should be personalized. Know why each of these items is in your pack and its main purpose: don't pack a pile of widgets just because it seems like a good idea. Give each item a hard look and leave it behind if something else you've already packed can do double duty. Some of the following items may already be in your first-aid kit:

❐ Pocket knife
❐ Nylon parachute cord (at least thirty feet)
❐ Strong thread and needles
❐ Rubber bands
❐ Large safety pins
❐ Wire twist-ties (good for replacing shoelaces)
❐ Spare buttons
❐ Duct tape (Just a few feet wrapped around a pencil— this works great for patching torn ponchos or packs.)
❐ Rubber glue (for shoe or tent repairs)
❐ Fishing line, hooks
❐ Matches in a waterproof container
❐ Water-purification tablets
❐ Firestarter and candles
❐ Flashlight with fresh batteries (Headlamps are very helpful, and keep your hands free.)
❐ Pouch to contain all of the above

Using This Guide

Understanding the Trail Descriptions

At the beginning of each trail description are short headings that are intended to give hikers a few at-a-glance details about the trail. Here is an explanation of each of these headings.

Main Attractions: Besides just getting into the great outdoors, most of us want to know specifically what is so great about a particular trail. This heading gives parents who haven't hiked the trail before some things to tell their kids to raise expectations a little.

Getting There: This tells you how to get to the trailhead. Usually the directions start from a well-known location, such as Moose, Wyoming, or Teton Village.

Trail Distance: This usually breaks down the trail distances to logical points and turnarounds.

Elevation Gain/Loss: This number, listed in feet, helps to given an idea of how much climbing you may be doing.

How Strenuous: This is broken down into three main categories: Easy, Moderate, and Strenuous. Also included

are recommendations as to what age groups should or shouldn't hike the trail. For example: Lunch Tree Hill is recommended for all age groups, but Green Lakes is not recommended for toddlers or preschoolers.

When to Go: This heading pinpoints the time a trail is clear of snow and mud and may be hiked until the snow falls again. Most mountain trails open up by July and close sometime in October. Valley trails usually open in late May and close by November. These times are generalizations: late or early storms can change things drastically. If you are hoping for an early- or late-season hike, your best bet is to check on current conditions at the park visitor center or the local Forest Service office.

Animals to Watch For: This is a short list of some of the animals most often spotted on a particular trail. It should be understood that many other animals are often seen. For instance, black bears, martens, owls, mink, field mice, and other animals are often present but are difficult to see, and therefore I don't always list them. Grizzly bears are rare south of the north end of Jackson Lake.

Maps and Information: This heading lists a map or pamphlet that may be obtained at a nearby visitor center.

Kid Comments: These are direct quotes of children's remarks during or after hiking that particular trail. Occasionally, I recorded comments I overheard from other people's children. (In the interests of honesty, I must say that I ignored negative comments and used only positive ones.) Sometimes I just had tout in more than one quote.

"Actually, I Liked All of Them But . . ."

All of the hikes in this book are good trails. There are no duds. Some may be very easy for your family, others a bit too hard. What may be the perfect trail for one family, may be so-so for another. But, to be honest, some are better than others. Rather than give you the author's opinion on which ones are best, I asked my children, who kid-tested all of the trails, which ones they thought were best. I asked them to pick out their favorites among three main categories: Short and easy walks, half-day hikes and all-day or overnight hikes.

Their answers surprised me a little. I think for some hikes the memories grow fonder with time. I hope your family will have the opportunity to hike most of these trails in this book and make their own list of favorites.

Short and easy walks:

Menor's Ferry. This trail was mentioned by all of my children as a favorite. I think the topper was the fresh-baked cookies in the general store.

Others mentioned as favorites were Swan Lake/Heron Pond, Teton Pass Trail and Rendezvous Mountain Trail.

Half-day hikes:

Jenny Lake/Hidden Falls/Inspiration Point. This was the clear winner among my children. They love the falls and the challenging hike up to Inspiration Point.

Other favorite trails include Taggart and Bradley Lakes, Leigh Lake, String Lake and Darby Canyon wind cave.

Long hikes and overnighters:

Death Canyon and Cascade Canyon/Lake Solitude. Both trails tie for the top honors in this category. Each of them has lots of wildlife and tremendous beauty with the added feature of nice campsites for overnight trips.

Another mentioned by the children as a favorite was Green Lakes.

A Word About Maps

There are several different maps covering the Teton Range. For many of the trails in this book, especially those in the "easy walks" section, you won't need anything more than the description map in this book. For other hikes it is recommended that you buy one of the many detailed maps available.

These large detailed maps come in handy in different ways. First, they help you get to the trailhead. Finding the trailhead can sometimes be the biggest challenge to doing the hike. Next, these maps add to the hike by helping identify what's around you. Knowing the names of peaks, streams, canyons and lakes that you are hiking past helps you make friends – just like knowing the names of people you meet. Maps also help you stay found. Although it's tough to become lost on the hikes in this book, having a map offers an extra bit of peace of mind. With the map, you can teach your children how to figure out where they are and where they are going.

Many of the maps listed below also have helpful historic, geological, and recreational information about the area.

Some of the maps are printed on both plastic and paper. I always buy plastic when it's available. A plastic map will last ten times longer and is well worth the extra dollar or two. Most of these maps are available at area bookstores, Forest Service visitor centers and at the national park book shops and visitor centers.

Here is a list of the maps for the area covered in this book, as well as notes explaining what kind of help they provide for the hiking family:

Earthwalk Press, Recreation Map, Grand Teton National Park. This topographic map covers the entire Teton Range, east and west, and all of the hikes in this book. It is available in paper and plastic.

Earthwalk Press, Hiking and Climbing Map, Grand Teton National Park. This topographic map covers only the mountains themselves. Available in paper and plastic.

United States Geological Survey Grand Teton National Park Map. A special-edition topographic map produced by the United State Geological Survey. Has a great deal of information on geology, history, plants, and animals. Available in plastic.

Trails Illustrated Grand Teton National Park Map. This topographic map covers the entire park and some of the west side of the Teton Range. Available only in plastic.

Jedediah Smith and Winegar Hole Wildernesses Targhee National Forest Map. This topographical map covers all of the west side of the Teton Range and some of the east side. Has good detail of the wilderness area. Available in paper and plastic.

Targhee National Forest Map, Island Park, Ashton, Teton Basin and Palisades Ranger Districts. Non-topographical map of the west side or "Idaho side" of the Teton range. Offers good information on campsites. Available only in paper.

Key to Symbols for Trail Activities and Amenities

Throughout this book, the following symbols are used to indicate the numerous activities and amenities you may find while exploring Teton area trails.

Handicap accessible

Fishing

Tram

Historic site

Mountain biking

Drinking water

Boating

Camping

Swimming

Wildlife

Canoeing

Horseback riding

Picnic tables

Restrooms

Teton Area Map

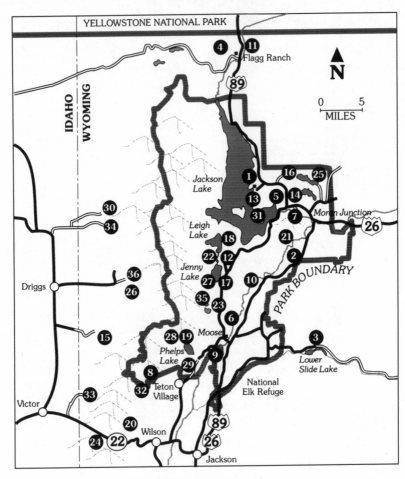

YELLOWSTONE NATIONAL PARK

Flagg Ranch

N

0   5
MILES

IDAHO

WYOMING

Jackson
Lake

Leigh
Lake

Jenny
Lake

Moran Junction

PARK BOUNDARY

Driggs

Moose

Phelps
Lake

Lower
Slide Lake

Teton
Village

National
Elk Refuge

Victor

Wilson

Jackson

Map legend

Lakes	⬭	**Park boundary**	▬▬▬
Rivers/Streams	∿	**State boundary**	— · — · —
Paved road	▬▬	**City/town**	—○—
Gravel/dirt road	∿∿	**Ranger station/**	
Main trail	- - - ⁓	**visitor's center**	⬆
Other trails	⁓⁓⁓	**Campground**	Λ
Trailhead	Ⓣ	**Mountain peak**	✕

Easy Walks and Short Hikes

In this chapter, families can expect to find walks that are less than an hour long and easy for everyone. These hikes are appropriate for toddlers and preschool children.

Colter Bay Lake Shore Trail

1

Main Attractions: Wildlife viewing, great scenery with Jackson Lake surrounded by the Tetons, and easy hiking

Getting There: From Jackson Lake Lodge, drive 4.5 miles northwest on Highway 89 to Colter Bay Village. Turn left (west) and drive to the end of the road; turn right, and park near the Colter Bay Visitor Center. The trail begins from the north end of the visitor center.

Trail Distance: 1.9 miles, round-trip

Elevation Gain/Loss: About 50 feet

How Strenuous: Easy. This is a good trip for all ages. Toddlers may need to be carried if the distance is too much.

When to Go: May through October for hiking. Skiing is available during the winter.

Animals to Watch For: Deer, moose, eagles, ospreys, waterfowl, songbirds, and small mammals (especially squirrels).

Maps and Information: Printed literature is available at the visitor center.

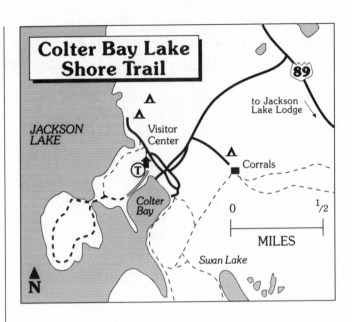

Colter Bay Lake Shore Trail

JACKSON LAKE

Visitor Center

to Jackson Lake Lodge

89

Corrals

Colter Bay

0   1/2

MILES

Swan Lake

N

Kid Comments

• • • • • • • • • • • •

I want to go down and see how cold the water is.

This trail once was a self-guided park nature trail complete with leaflets and signs. Now the signs are gone, but the trail continues to offer beautiful views of the lake, its shore, and the mountains across the lake.

After leaving the visitor center, you will follow a paved walk on the north side of the marina for about .3 miles. After about a half-mile, you will come to a narrow land bridge that takes you out to an island in the lake. The trail offers mostly easy hiking. The uphill climbs are few, short, and not very steep. The area is forested mostly by lodgepole pines.

At the far west end, the trail breaks through the forest and opens up to views of the lake and mountains beyond. There are also a few side trails around the island that lead down to the water.

The prominent square-topped peak across the lake is Mount Moran. Looking south from Mount Moran is Teewinot Mountain and Grand Teton. North of Mount Moran is Bivouac Peak and Eagles Rest Peak. The canyon just north of Eagles Rest Peak has two huge

waterfalls. From the west shore of Jackson Lake you should be able to see at least one of these falls.

During the summer, watch for pelicans, ducks, and other waterfowl in the water near the shore. On land, keep an eye out for red squirrels and ground squirrels. Deer and moose are occasional visitors to the island area.

The trail circles the island and returns back to the land bridge. Another trail follows the lakeshore going north. This trail passes by the Colter Bay Amphitheater and returns to the road.

Colter Bay was formed after Jackson Lake Dam was built in 1916, raising the lake's level more than thirty feet. The bay was named after John Colter, a fur trapper who traveled through the valley during the winter of 1807–1808. Colter is believed to be the first white man to visit Jackson Hole. He was a part of the Lewis and Clark Expedition but was discharged before the return trip in hopes of establishing a fur-trading operation in the region.

Moose are usually found close to water. They are dark brown. The males have flat antlers with small prongs projecting forward. Moose are the largest deer in the world— some can be 7 feet tall and weigh up to 1,400 pounds.

Final Thoughts

A pamphlet available at the Colter Bay Visitor Center will be very helpful as you find your way around the maze of trails in this area. You can also purchase an expanded trail guide for the Colter Bay Area at the park's visitor centers.

There are also ranger-conducted activities and walks in this area. Check at the visitor center for schedules. The visitor center is open from May through September.

Cunningham Cabin

2

Main Attractions: An old turn-of-the-century homestead cabin and ranch plot. Easy interpretive trail.

Getting There: The trail lies on the east side of the
Snake River between Moose Junction and Moran
Junction, on Highway 89. Drive north of the Moose
Junction on Highway 89 about 12.5 miles. Watch
for the signs for Cunningham Cabin. The site is just
north of Triangle X Ranch. There is a large parking
lot just off the highway for vehicles pulling trailers.
Cars can drive down the road a bit and park next to
the property.

Trail Distance: .75-mile

Elevation Gain/Loss: 20 feet

How Strenuous: Easy. Recommended for all ages.

When to Go: May through September

Animals to Watch For: Ground squirrels, badgers, eagles, coyotes, songbirds. Bison are often seen in the
neighborhood.

Maps and Information: An excellent park pamphlet
is available at the beginning of the trail. The pamphlet contains old photos of J. Pierce Cunningham
and his wife, Margaret. It also has a photo of their
ranchhouse, which no longer exists. The pamphlet
is free and usually at the trailhead by May.

For this walk, tell your children to use their imagination to see barns, corrals, horses in their stalls, and
ranch hands working with the cows and horses. Besides
the one cabin, all that remains at the ranch are the
buck-and-rail fences and dimly outlined foundations with
a few stones and broken posts.

Tell your children to imagine living here, where winter
snow comes in November and doesn't leave until April.
The usual winter temperatures hover right around zero.

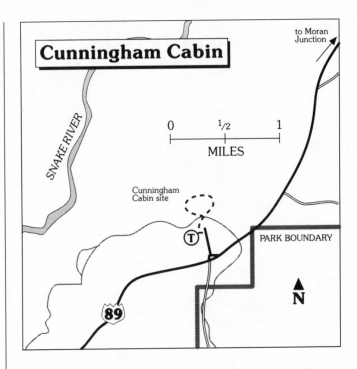

Cunningham Cabin

to Moran Junction

SNAKE RIVER

0   1/2   1
MILES

Cunningham Cabin site

T

PARK BOUNDARY

N

89

The Cunninghams spent forty years in Jackson Hole, struggling to make their cattle ranch pay. Eventually, they left for greener pastures in Idaho in 1928. The Cunningham cabin, the only building now standing, was a temporary residence until the ranchhouse was built in 1895. The old cabin was converted into a barn and blacksmith shop.

The Cunningham property was the scene of one of Jackson Hole's most famous violent affairs. In 1892 Pierce Cunningham sold hay to two strangers—Montana wranglers George Spencer and Mike Burnett—for their herd of horses. He allowed them to winter in his cabin while he stayed at another cabin on Flat Creek. Rumor had it that the two men had stolen their horses. Cunningham checked out the brands on the animals but couldn't be certain. Two men claiming to be U.S. marshals on the trail of Montana horse thieves snowshoed into Jackson from Idaho over Teton Pass. They gathered

Children love to explore the inside of the historic Cunningham Cabin.

up a posse of eight men and surrounded the cabin. Cunningham refused to participate. Spencer and Burnett were killed by shotgun and rifle fire. The speculation that the two men were horse thieves was never proved.

Most of Jackson Hole's ranches eventually converted from cattle to "dude." Dude ranches catered to easterners seeking excitement in Wyoming's stunning scenery. You can imagine how easy it might be to slip away from your summer chores on the ranch and ride the short distance to a favorite fishing hole on the Snake River.

Final Thoughts

There are lots of ground squirrels throughout the trail area. Remind children not to feed any of the wildlife, even if they see other children doing it.

Kid Comments
....
The people must have been short to live in this cabin.

3 | Gros Ventre Slide Nature Trail

Main Attractions: Fun interpretive trail, swimming, fishing, wildlife-viewing

Getting There: Drive 6 miles north of Jackson on Highway 89; turn right (east) at the Gros Ventre Junction. Drive 1 mile past the community of Kelly and turn right (east); drive about 5 miles to the Gros Ventre Slide display.

Trail Distance: .4-miles

Elevation Gain/Loss: About 50 feet

How Strenuous: Easy. Recommended for the whole family.

When to Go: Early May through October.

Animals to Watch For: Waterfowl, deer, eagles, ground squirrels, pikas, and marmots

This short interpretive trail gives hikers a close-up view of what happens when huge geologic forces decide to cut loose.

In June 1925, an entire side of Sheep Mountain slid down into the Gros Ventre (pronounced *grow-vaunt*) Canyon and dammed the Gros Ventre River. The slide was one of the largest earth movements to be seen in the world. Just before the slide occurred, heavy rains had been soaking the area, and it is speculated that earthquake tremors helped set off the monster slide. Geologists estimate that nearly 50 million cubic yards of sandstone poured down the mountain and blocked the half-mile wide canyon to a depth of 225 feet. The rock and debris piled several hundred feet up the far side of the canyon. Witnesses said the slide took only a few minutes. A mile-long, two-thousand-feet-wide scar still remains on the north side of Sheep Mountain.

The new dam backed up the river and flooded roads and ranches. Seepage through the dam increased until it equaled normal river flow. Engineers at the time believed

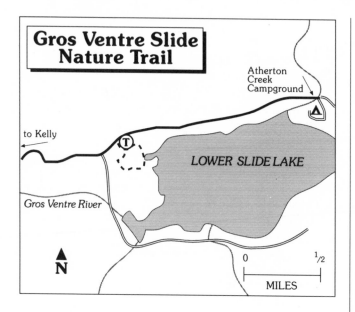

Gros Ventre Slide Nature Trail

Atherton Creek Campground

to Kelly

LOWER SLIDE LAKE

Gros Ventre River

N

0   1/2

MILES

the earthen dam would hold, but in 1927 a wet spring backed up the water behind the dam even higher. On May 18, the upper sixty feet or so of the dam broke loose. A flood of muddy, rocky water poured down the canyon. Six people were killed as the town of Kelly, 3.5 miles away, was nearly washed away. Livestock were killed, ranch lands were covered in a layer of mud and debris, and buildings were destroyed.

Today the four-mile-long lake is used for wind surfing, canoeing, camping, and fishing.

The trail starts near the restrooms just down from the display overlooking the slide. The Forest Service has a sign posted about every thirty to fifty yards identifying common trees, shrubs, geologic sites, and various phenomena caused by the slide. There are also signs to keep you on the right path. At the far end of the loop, near the water, there are a few benches to sit on and take in the view of the lake. This is a good trail to take to help you learn tree and bush varieties.

Kid Comments
....

Those must have been tall trees if you can see them sticking up out of the water.

We found a lot of evidence of moose passing through the area. There is also an old beaver lodge along the water's edge. If you bring along binoculars, look for waterfowl and ospreys patrolling the water.

Out in the water are remnants of the old forest standing neck-deep in the lake. These trees are fun to canoe out to. They also serve to frustrate many a fisherman.

Final Thoughts

On the way back to Kelly, just inside the park boundary, there is a large pond beside the road that is fed by a warm spring. This is called Kelly Warm Spring and is a great place to stop for a swim. The water is eighty degrees year-round. There's plenty of parking and a toilet on the north side of the road. Watch out for slippery rocks along the edge of the water.

Huckleberry Hot Springs Trail

Main Attractions: Soaking in a hot natural spring, wildlife-viewing, and a short easy hike

Getting There: From Jackson Lake Lodge, drive 20 miles north on Highway 89 to the Snake River Bridge on the John D. Rockefeller Jr. Memorial Parkway. Drive past the bridge about .5 mile and turn left at the sign for Flagg Ranch/Grassy Lake. Turn right at the Flagg Ranch headquarters and continue on this road about .5 mile. When you cross a small bridge over Polecat Creek, park your car. The trail is marked by a rail and small sign to keep out motor vehicles. The trail heads due north.

Another trail also leads out of the campground next to Flagg Ranch. This trail follows along the east side of Polecat Creek. This is a better trail to take if you go in the winter on cross-country skis. Depending on where you start walking, this can add an extra one-quarter to one-half mile to the hike. This trail follows the east side of Polecat Creek on an old paved road.

Trail Distance: About 1 mile one way

Elevation Gain/Loss: 10 to 20 feet up or down

How Strenuous: Easy. Recommended for all ages.

When to Go: Year-round. When the snow flies this is a popular destination for cross-country skiers.

Animals to Watch For: Moose, deer, small mammals, songbirds, beaver, bear, and waterfowl.

This is a very easy hike with a fun destination. Bring along your swimsuits.

How you approach this hike depends on the time of year. If you go in summer, I strongly recommend that you go early in the morning—the earlier the better. This can prove a challenge for sleepy kids, but tell them they'll be soaking in nature's bathtub. The reasons for

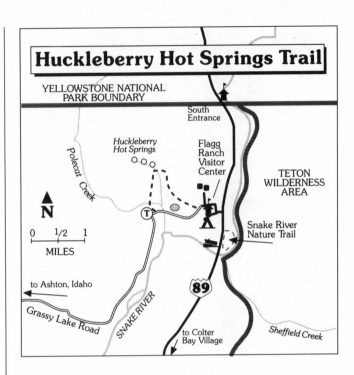

Huckleberry Hot Springs Trail

YELLOWSTONE NATIONAL
PARK BOUNDARY

South
Entrance

Huckleberry
Hot Springs

Flagg
Ranch
Visitor
Center

Polecat Creek

TETON
WILDERNESS
AREA

N

Snake River
Nature Trail

0   1/2   1

MILES

to Ashton, Idaho

Grassy Lake Road

SNAKE RIVER

89

to Colter
Bay Village

Sheffield Creek

Kid Comments

OOH! This
water really
is warm!

going at the crack of dawn are two. First, early in the morning the air is much cooler and a warm soak is nice —later in the day when the temperature climbs to eighty-five degrees, jumping into hundred-degree water is hardly refreshing. Second, mosquitoes are less active in the early morning. Another possible option is to go after dusk, when the temperature drops after the sun sets. If you go at this time, be sure to take a flashlight, and be certain you know where you're going.

If you go on this hike in the spring or fall, the trip can be heavenly, especially on a cold day.

The trail follows an old road that takes you through thick lodgepole pine forest. After about .4-mile, the trail crosses Polecat Creek. In the spring the water can be over your knees.

The trail along the east side of Polecat Creek passes ponds and sloughs regulated by beavers. Ducks, geese,

Easy Walks and Short Hikes

One of the largest pools at Huckleberry Hot Springs. It features knee-deep water and will seat several people.

and swans are often seen in this area. You may also spot tunnels along the banks of the water. These burrows are used by beavers and muskrats in lieu of a lodge. The tunnels are dug below the water level and up into the bank of the stream or pond. In late summer, when the water levels drop and expose the burrows, the animals often find new accommodations.

When you get to the warm creek, put your hand in and feel the warm water.

Walk upstream to some pools created by former visitors stacking rocks. You'll notice that tiny hot springs pop up all along the creek. The farther up the creek you go, the hotter the springs seem to get. One large pool has a small fall pouring in hot water, and it seats a large family comfortably in about two feet of water. This pool is well over one hundred degrees in temperature.

Pick out the pool that suits you and enjoy a fine soak.

Final Thoughts

Be prepared for the possibility of meeting skinny-dippers. The area is managed by the Park Service, and it makes regular checkups on the hot-springs area. Its main concern is that all trash is picked up, especially food and food containers. It doesn't want the leftover garbage attracting bears. Because the area is considered backcountry, rangers also check to see if the "no dog" rule is being followed.

Lunch Tree Hill Nature Trail

5

Main Attractions: Easy nature walk with great views of Jackson Lake and the Teton Range beyond; a great view of an expansive marsh area between the Jackson Lake Lodge and the lake; signs identifying plants and animals

Getting There: Drive 1 mile north of the Jackson Lake junction on Highway 89 and turn left (west) into the Jackson Lake Lodge area. Park near the lodge. Walk into the lodge, which is a sight to see in and of itself, and exit out the back near the large picture window facing the Teton Range. Turn right and start the hike at the sign "Lunch Tree Hill Loop Trail."

Trail Distance: .4-mile if you just stick to the paved path. Add another .5-mile if you take some of the dirt paths around the bluff.

Elevation Gain/Loss: 100 feet up and down

How Strenuous: Easy. Recommended for all ages.

When to Go: April through October

Animals to Watch For: Moose, sandhill cranes, beavers, waterfowl, small mammals, and songbirds

Lunch Tree Hill rises above the very large and marshy willow flat east of Jackson Lake. Mount Moran and the rest of the Teton Range serve as a dramatic backdrop. The view from Lunch Tree Hill Trail is picture-postcard quality.

But this is also a superior wildlife-viewing trail. Don't forget to keep your binoculars ready, because this is one of the best trails from which to spot a moose. As you walk along the lake side of the trail, look out across the marsh. From this vantage point you can often spot sandhill cranes, beaver lodges and canals, and other water-loving animals. The moose feed on the willows and other wetland plants. Despite weighing up to nine hundred

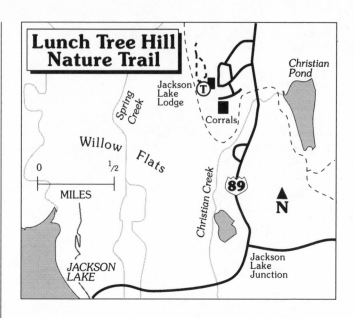

Lunch Tree Hill Nature Trail

Christian Pond

Jackson Lake Lodge

T

Corrals

Spring Creek

Willow Flats

Christian Creek

89

0   ½

MILES

N

JACKSON LAKE

Jackson Lake Junction

pounds, they seem to blend in well with their surroundings.

Lunch Tree Hill is an interesting contrast with the marsh below. The bluff is covered with such arid-environment plants as sagebrush, plus a few lodgepole pines and a small cluster of aspen.

The paved trail features descriptive signs of plants and animals. These signs are a big help in assisting children to learn the names of plants. At the turnaround point of the trail is a large rock with a plaque honoring the contributions of John D. Rockefeller Jr. in getting the valley floor next to the Tetons included in the national park.

There are well-defined informal trails that continue around the bluff. These trails can get you a bit closer to a large pond on the northwest side of the hill. Look for waterfowl in these wetter areas.

Try this trail early in the morning or just before dusk. The lighting on the mountains offers a more dramatic view then, and these times are also excellent for viewing wildlife.

Final Thoughts

This is a good place to visit if you are in the area during hunting season in the fall because it is off-limits to firearms. Elk, moose, and other animals are often present in higher numbers to avoid hunting pressures elsewhere in the area.

Menor's Ferry Trail

6

Main Attractions: A glimpse into the past with a short walk through a picturesque turn-of-the-century homestead. Also, free ferry rides across the river during certain times of the week.

Getting There: From the Moose Visitor Center, drive west through the park entrance gate, and take the first right after the entrance gate. Drive to the end of the short road and park in the parking lot near the Chapel of the Transfiguration. The trail begins on the east side (toward the river) of the parking lot.

Trail Distance: .5-mile round-trip

Elevation Gain/Loss: Basically flat

How Strenuous: Easy. Recommended for all ages. Much of the route is accessible to the wheelchair-bound.

When to Go: June through September. Check at the Moose Visitor Center for a schedule of ferry operation.

Animals to Watch For: Songbirds, eagles, waterfowl in the river, deer, moose, and elk

Maps and Information: A free informative handout at the trailhead guides you along the path and tells you about historic features and landmarks

This trail is very interesting and just plain fun. The once-elaborate homestead of William D. Menor included barns, a smithy, a general store, a garden, irrigated hay fields, pastures, a whitewashed cabin, a smokehouse, sheds, and a ferry across the river. Menor's Ferry became a vital crossing for early settlers in Jackson Hole. He charged twenty-five cents for horse and rider to cross. Today you can cross on the ferry for free.

The restored homestead helps visitors picture what life was like about one hundred years ago. Most of the

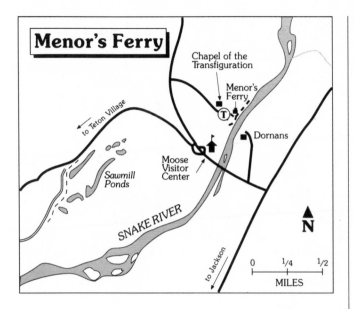

Menor's Ferry

Chapel of the Transfiguration

Menor's Ferry

to Teton Village

Sawmill Ponds

Moose Visitor Center

Dornans

SNAKE RIVER

to Jackson

N

0   1/4   1/2
MILES

buildings are open. Inside you will find displays, old relics, and photos from the past.

One of the highlights of the trail is Menor's home and general store. During the summer, a Park Service worker operates the store and sells candy and trinkets. The shopkeeper also showed us around the back rooms. Particularly fascinating was the elk-horn chair and straw-tick-mattress bed. On our visit, the children got a sampling of gingersnaps fresh out of the hot woodstove oven.

Near the general store is a root cellar, a privy, a well, and the ferry. Tell the children to try to picture the entire scene under three or four feet of snow. And how about the trip to the privy when it's twenty below zero and the wind is blowing?

On the far south end of the trail is the Maude Noble cabin. This cabin was moved onto the Menor homestead in 1918, when Noble purchased the land. The entire area was later purchased by John D. Rockefeller and eventually donated to the park.

Kid Comments

I like the old photographs of people going over Teton Pass in the winter.

Children investigate a replica of Menor's Ferry docked on the banks of the Snake River. Early settlers used a similar ferry to cross the river. The park offers rides on the ferry during the summer months.

Today, inside the cabin is a wonderful photo display of early life in Jackson Hole. The photos are grouped by various themes, such as wildlife or transportation. The old-timey dress and cars should provide lots of fun for the children. Dad enjoyed the pictures of large catches of trout.

Final Thoughts

After you make the trail's circuit, don't forget to visit the historic log Chapel of the Transfiguration. During the summer, Episcopal meetings are held there each Sunday. The chapel is open for visitors throughout the week. A very nice view of one of God's creations, the Teton Range, is seen through a picture window behind the pulpit.

Oxbow Bend

Main Attractions: Wildlife-viewing, getting wet, fishing, and easy short trails

Getting There: Drive 3.2 miles north of Moran Junction and turn left (south) on an unmarked road. After a short distance the road becomes dirt. Drive to the end, about a mile, and park near the bridge over the river.

Trail Distance: From .25- to .4-mile, depending on how much exploring you want to do

Elevation Gain/Loss: 10 feet

How Strenuous: Easy. Recommended for all ages. Be careful with little ones around the water, though.

When to Go: Late May to October

Animals to Watch For: Waterfowl, deer, moose, elk, eagles, songbirds, beavers, otters, and other small mammals.

This is a great destination for a family picnic on a blanket with the availability of easy walks, wildlife-viewing and fishing spots. The Oxbow Bend area is a section of the Snake River that resembles a pioneer's oxbow. The bend was formed after the large meander was cut off from the main stream when the river took a more direct path. The area is home to geese, pelicans, swans, herons, ducks, eagles, ospreys, otters, deer, and moose.

There are two directions I recommend for exploring by foot. The first path is on the other side of the wooden bridge. As you walk over the bridge, look down into the clear water on the upstream side for fish. Most of the fish you spot will be whitefish. Some of these fish can be two feet long. My children love to walk up and down the bridge and point out the fish to each other saying, "Hey, come see this one. It's huge!"

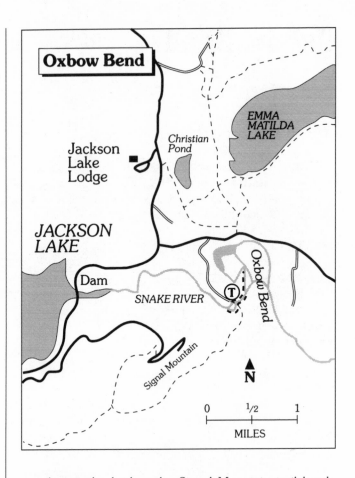

Across the bridge, the Signal Mountain trail heads off through the thick lodgepole pine forest on its way to the Signal Mountain Lodge. Although mostly flat and easy, this trail is uneventful. Instead, when you cross the bridge, follow the easy trail along the slow-moving Snake River backwater to your right. This side channel has a small island in its center. The backwater area is often a haven to waterfowl. The trail circles around to the inlet of this side channel. At times the trail follows along a steep bank. You may want to hold small children's hands so that a misstep doesn't lead to an unexpected swim.

Children can spot fish in the Snake River from Cattleman's Bridge at Oxbow Bend.

The second direction to hike is back on the other side of the bridge. Follow the river downstream to a channel, and follow the bank along a peninsula that pokes out into the large slack water of the Oxbow Bend. This informal trail is often used by fishermen. The paths in this area can be followed for more than a half-mile.

If you are serious about doing some fishing, look for places where fast water meets slow water, drop-offs near gravel bars, and underwater ledges. Fish also rest behind rocks in the riffles and runs where the water isn't too deep.

If children want to get wet, don't let them go into flowing water deeper than their knees. The Snake River is not a tame river.

Final Thoughts

The section of the river from the Jackson Lake Dam to Oxbow Bend is popular with canoers. Below Oxbow Bend the river becomes nastier and is navigated mostly by rafts and Mackenzie River boats.

Kid Comments
. . . .
Look at those huge fish! They're everywhere by this bridge.

Rendezvous Mountain Tram Walk

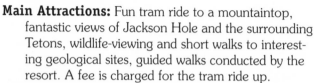

Main Attractions: Fun tram ride to a mountaintop, fantastic views of Jackson Hole and the surrounding Tetons, wildlife-viewing and short walks to interesting geological sites, guided walks conducted by the resort. A fee is charged for the tram ride up.

Getting There: Drive west on Highway 22 from Jackson, turn right on the Teton Village Road, and follow the signs to the Jackson Hole ski area. Park in the lot near the tram.

Trail Distance: .2-mile if you walk the paths near the tram; .5-mile if you head down the Rendezvous Mountain Trail for a short distance.

Elevation Gain/Loss: The elevation at the top of Rendezvous Mountain is 10,450 feet. The paths around the top gain about 20 feet; the path loses elevation quickly as you go down the mountain road—about 150 feet down to the first switchback.

How Strenuous: Easy if you stay around the top. Moderate if you walk down to the Rendezvous Mountain road. The top area is appropriate for all age groups. Keep in mind that quick elevation gains can be hard for some very small children to adjust to.

When to Go: A clear day from late June to early October

Animals to Watch For: Most of the big animals to be seen on this trip are only visible during the tram ride up and down. Look for moose, deer, bears, foxes, songbirds, and small mammals.

Maps and Information: The ski resort has information specialists on duty during the day at the snack bar.

It's hard to compete with a tram ride that takes you 4,000 vertical feet up. But the view from the summit of Rendezvous Mountain is tremendous.

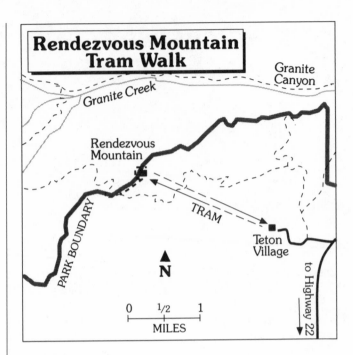

Rendezvous Mountain Tram Walk

Granite Canyon

Granite Creek

Rendezvous Mountain

TRAM

Teton Village

PARK BOUNDARY

to Highway 22

N

0   1/2   1
MILES

Kid Comments

We saw four moose on the ride up.

Wow! I can really see the tops of the mountains now.

Once you step off the tram, two things immediately assault your senses. The first is that it is much cooler at 10,450 feet than it is back on the valley floor. The temperature can easily be twenty to thirty degrees colder, so come prepared with a sweater or windbreaker. The other assault on the senses is visual. You can see more than fifty miles on a clear day. The sight of Jackson Hole far below will fascinate children and adults. Remember to bring along a pair of binoculars.

There is no formal route to hike at the top of the tram, but there are paths that take you to different viewpoints on the mountaintop. You will notice that the vegetation at this altitude is stunted and tiny. This is alpine tundra country. Anything that grows here is blasted by fierce winter weather. Trees are few and stunted, the growing season is very short. Signs admonish people to stay on the trails to give what few plants do grow here a fighting chance.

The short trails from the tram take you to the summit and along nearby viewpoints. Keep an eye on children who like to stray, because the mountainsides drop abruptly in places. Dangerous areas are marked with signs and ropes.

At the top of the summit is an observation area, with signs to identify surrounding peaks and a coin-operated telescope. This vantage point offers great views of Grand Teton and other Teton crest peaks. It's easy to burn up a lot of film up here. Remember to take some shots of the family on the mountaintop.

Walk south of the snack-bar area for some great views of the Snake River and the Gros Ventre Range to the east. I tell the kids to try and imagine this country before there were any highways or houses or even people. Another fun thing to imagine is what the valley looked like when glaciers crawled down out of the mountain canyons and into Jackson Hole, several thousand years ago.

Final Thoughts

Short guided hikes are usually conducted here twice a day during the summer. These hikes start near the snack bar and head down the road to a rocky bowl about .25-mile to the south. The guides are resort employees who are knowledgeable about the area's geology, flora, and fauna. Check at the tram office before going up, or at the mountaintop snack bar for schedules of these guided hikes.

9 Sawmill Ponds Overlook

Main Attractions: Wildlife-viewing and easy walking
Getting There: From Moose Village, take the Moose-Wilson Road south. The turnoff for this road is just west of the visitor center. Drive 1.2 miles south and park at the pullout on the left (east) side of the road. The trail starts on the south end of the parking area. Do not hike down into the pond area—this is sensitive wildlife habitat.
Trail Distance: .6-mile round-trip
Elevation Gain/Loss: Flat
How Strenuous: Easy. Recommended for all ages.
When to Go: Late May through October
Animals to Watch For: Moose, deer, elk, waterfowl, songbirds, beavers, and small mammals

This is an easy trail that follows along the top of a high steep bank. From the vantage point at the top of this bank, hikers can look over the streams and ponds below. Have your cameras and binoculars ready on this hike. In the early morning or late evening, when many animals are most active, moose and deer are often seen near the water. There is an interpretive sign at the center of the parking area explaining why moose find this habitat so attractive.

Although there are trails heading down to the water, please don't walk near the water. Park officials want to keep this sensitive wildlife habitat from being disturbed by people.

After you walk south along the trail about .2-mile, you will see a large pond directly east. You can expect to see a variety of waterfowl here throughout the summer. Bring along binoculars or a camera with a telephoto lens to pick out individual species of duck, goose, and other waterfowl. We noticed an old beaver lodge in the largest pond.

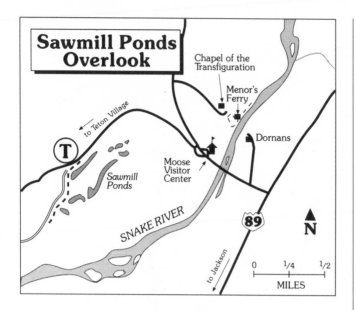

Sawmill Ponds Overlook

Chapel of the Transfiguration

Menor's Ferry

Dornans

to Teton Village

Moose Visitor Center

Sawmill Ponds

SNAKE RIVER

to Jackson

89

N

0   1/4   1/2
MILES

There are a few large trees along the trail that can offer shade on hot days. This trail is a good place to teach children an old Boy Scout trick for observing wildlife. Find a log or stump or tree trunk in a nice shady spot, and sit. After you sit motionless and silent for about five minutes, the nearby animals begin to accept you as part of the environment. This is a great way to observe songbirds and squirrels. Occasionally, you get a bonus with the passing of a deer, moose, or other large animal.

The trail ends a hundred yards or so past the big pond. A gravel road continues on to an unpaved landing strip.

Final Thoughts

The Moose-Wilson Road is famous for its wildlife. I have never traveled this road during the morning or evening hours and not seen wildlife. Because the road is curvy and unpaved part of the way, you have to drive it fairly slowly. The slower speed gives you more chances

Kid Comments
••••••••••••••

There are sure a lot of ducks down there.

Sawmill Ponds is a very good place to sit and observe waterfowl and other wildlife.

to spot deer and moose. Drive this road first thing in the morning and you're almost sure to see a deer or two. More often than not, you will spot a moose. Sometimes it helps to assign eyes for the left and eyes for the right side of the car. Tell children to look for two things: movement and color. Movement is helpful for spotting deer. Looking for color, specifically dark chocolate brown, helps your eye pick out moose.

10 Schwabacher's Landing

Main Attractions: Beaver structures, fishing, wildlife-viewing, and easy hiking in a different environment

Getting There: Drive 4 miles north of Moose Junction on Highway 89. Turn left (west) at the sign for Schwabacher's Landing. Follow the dirt road down to the river about 1.5 miles; it ends at a parking lot.

Trail Distance: 2 to 4 miles round-trip, depending on how far you wish to wander

Elevation Gain/Loss: 20 feet up or down

How Strenuous: Easy. Recommended for all ages for a short distance.

When to Go: May to October. Avoid this area during hunting season.

Animals to Watch For: Moose, deer, beavers, muskrats, otters, elk, coyotes, small mammals, songbirds, waterfowl, eagles, and occasionally bison

If all you've seen so far of the national park are the mountain areas, here's a fun change of pace. The hiking is easy and there are some classic beaver dams and lodges to capture a family's imagination.

As you walk through this river area you will notice that willows and cottonwoods predominate. Thick undergrowth allows for moose and other animals to disappear after only a few steps. A few dozen yards from the water and the land turns to sagebrush.

Schwabacher's Landing is a popular boat launch for anglers and river rafters on the Snake River. It's also a popular starting point for anglers fishing on foot. Right near the parking area is a very large beaver dam and a lodge on the far side. If you walk upstream from the parking area, you will come upon a few more beaver dams. Before the days of the trapper, beaver used to do their work during the day. Now they are mostly nocturnal, but

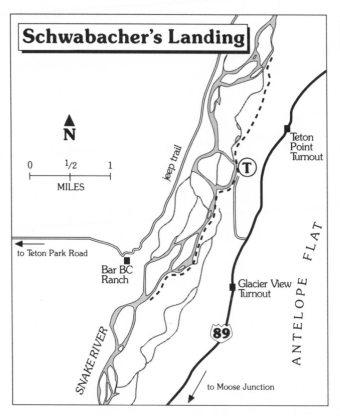

Schwabacher's Landing

N

0   1/2   1
MILES

jeep trail

(T)

Teton
Point
Turnout

to Teton Park Road

Bar BC
Ranch

Glacier View
Turnout

89

ANTELOPE FLAT

SNAKE RIVER

to Moose Junction

occasionally one can be spotted in the early morning or
late evening.

A trail, used by wildlife as much as by people, heads
out over the sagebrush for about 1.5 miles to another
set of islands and channels that are visited less. If you
head this far north, be prepared to do a little bush-
whacking. Small herds of elk or bison can quickly create
a maze of trails. But with the river on the west side and
the sagebrush flats on the east side, it's very difficult to
become lost. These islands and channels offer great opportunities to land one of the river's famous cutthroat
trout. Most of the trout will be lying along gravel bars
and eddy lines. Fish the areas where fast water meets
slow water and behind obstructions such as fallen logs,
rocks, or underwater drop-offs.

One of the main features at Schwabacher's Landing is a very large beaver pond.

If you feel the urge to cross the water, my rule of thumb is never to let children (or adults) go into fast water deeper than their knees. If you slip and fall into water deeper than this, it is very difficult to regain your footing in the swift current. Each year the river claims a few lives; mostly boaters and rafters.

Downstream from the parking area about .75-mile is another set of islands and gravel bars. As can be deduced from the trail, these seem to receive more visitors.

One animal you might spot if you are fishing is the river otter. Otters are super swimmers and phenomenal fishers. It seems when the fishing is slow for humans, they will hang around catching fish after fish just to show us up. Their preferred method is to swim upstream underwater and catch the fish from behind (fish always face upstream). Then the otter will float down-stream on its back, eating the fish. If there are more fish to be caught, an otter will repeat this process several times in the same section of river. Watching otters is a rare thrill. They seem to have a preference for whitefish, but they also eat trout.

Final Thoughts

Water levels fluctuate according to how much is being released from the dam. By late summer the water levels are usually several feet lower, and some side channels may be completely dry.

Kid Comments
....

That's a big beaver dam. Are you sure people didn't help?

11 Snake River Nature Trail

Main Attractions: Easy, self-guided nature trail; nice views of the Snake River; wildlife-viewing; opportunities to fish

Getting There: From Colter Bay, drive north 15 miles on Highway 89. Cross the Snake River Bridge and park on the left (west) side of the highway in the boat launch parking lot. The trail is on the east side of the road about .25-mile south of Flagg Ranch. Look for the post with a small box containing leaflets.

Trail Distance: .5-mile

Elevation Gain/Loss: Basically flat

How Strenuous: Easy. Recommended for all ages. Be careful crossing the highway.

When to Go: May through late October

Animals to Watch For: Songbirds, moose, small mammals, beavers, deer, and waterfowl

Maps and Information: The leaflet that guides you along the trail is all you will need

This trail gives you nice views of the Snake River where it's still a youngster. This river originates less than thirty miles away.

Another interesting sight along the trail is the large skeleton forest on the other side of the river. The dead trees are the result of the huge Huck Fire that ignited on August 20, 1988. The fire started when a windstorm blew a tree across a power line. Sparks from the power line set the dry forest on fire. Massive efforts to put out the fire were futile, and ninety thousand acres were burned before fall snows finally snuffed the flames.

The trail takes you along the river and through willow brush, grasses, and sagebrush. Numbered posts along the way explain much of the habitat. For such a small area, there is a large diversity in habitat here.

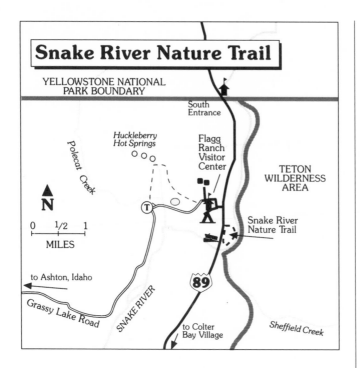

Snake River Nature Trail

YELLOWSTONE NATIONAL PARK BOUNDARY

South Entrance

Huckleberry Hot Springs

Flagg Ranch Visitor Center

TETON WILDERNESS AREA

Polecat Creek

N

0   1/2   1

MILES

Snake River Nature Trail

to Ashton, Idaho

Grassy Lake Road

SNAKE RIVER

89

to Colter Bay Village

Sheffield Creek

If you take this trail at dawn or dusk, your chances of seeing wildlife are increased.

If this short trail whets your appetite for more, you can extend your walk along the water near the bridge. This is good fishing water, but it receives a lot of pressure from anglers. If you are serious about fishing, you may want to walk a way up- or downstream to find holes that aren't hit so often.

Final Thoughts

Fishing is usually best during the early summer. As the water levels drop during the late summer, many of the fish migrate down to Jackson Lake.

Kid Comments
• • • • • • • • • • • • •
That must have been a big fire to kill all those trees.

12 | String Lake Paved Trail

Main Attractions: Beautiful views of String Lake and the mountains beyond, wildlife-viewing, swimming, and easy walking

Getting There: Drive 14 miles north of Jackson on Highway 89 to Moose Junction. Turn left (west) and drive 11 miles to the North Jenny Lake Junction and turn left (west). Drive 2.5 miles to the String Lake picnic area and park at the parking lot near the restrooms.

Trail Distance: About .4-mile round-trip

Elevation Gain/Loss: Basically flat

How Strenuous: Easy. Recommended for all ages. Strollers and wheelchairs work fine here.

When to Go: May to October

Animals to Watch For: Small mammals, ospreys, moose, elk, deer, songbirds, and waterfowl

During the summer of 1994, park trail crews hauled tons of asphalt on the backs of mules along the trail on the east side of String Lake. When the dust finally settled, a new trail was born. This trail is tailor-made for visitors who want great scenery and easy walking. Strollers, wheelchairs, and sandaled feet are all easily accommodated by the paved walk.

The walk begins near the Leigh Lake trailhead on the north end of the picnic area. The trail parallels the narrow lake. In many places you are only a few steps from the water. There are some benches along the walk for sitting and soaking up the view. These benches are made of split lodgepole pine and fit in well with the surroundings.

If it is a hot day, you may want to don swimsuits and go wading. Be forewarned that the water can be pretty darn cold. Canoeing is also a popular activity at String Lake. The paved trail ends near the canoe launch parking lot.

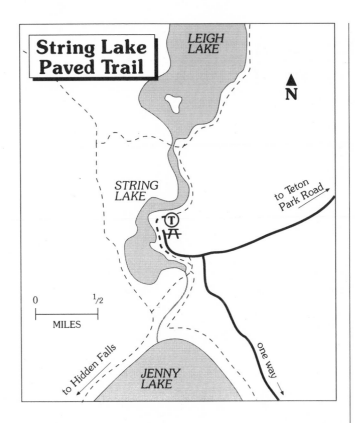

String Lake
Paved Trail

LEIGH
LAKE

N

STRING
LAKE

to Teton
Park Road

T

0   ¹/₂

MILES

to Hidden Falls

JENNY
LAKE

one way

If your tribe wants to go a little farther, you can walk about another .25-mile past the canoe launch area to a bridge across the String Lake outlet. The bridge is at the trailhead for the Jenny Lake and String Lake trails.

Final Thoughts

Look for red squirrels and ground squirrels along the path. Remind your children not to feed the critters. Deer and moose are often in the neighborhood early in the morning or late in the day.

Kid Comments
• • • • • • • • • • • • •

I like these benches. I wish we had some like this at home.

Nice benches and picnic tables are placed along the paved trail at String Lake.

Swan Lake/ Heron Pond

13

Main Attractions: Superior wildlife-viewing opportunities, especially in the early morning and just before dusk; an easy trail and opportunities to fish

Getting There: Go north on Highway 89 from Moran Junction for about 9 miles. Go to the end of the road and turn left at the visitor center. The trailhead is on the south end of the parking lot. There is also a connecting trail leading from the tent-cabin area just off the road that leads to the horse corrals.

Trail Distance: It's about 1.4 miles from the marina trailhead to the south end of Swan Lake; the return trip along Heron Pond is also 1.4 miles.

Elevation Gain/Loss: 6,780 feet at the trailhead; the trail gains and loses only about 50 feet over its distance

How Strenuous: Easy. Recommended for all ages.

When to Go: June to October for hiking and horseback riding; late November to April for winter activities. Before Memorial Day and after Labor Day, you'll probably have the trails all to yourself.

Animals to Watch For: Moose, elk, deer, small mammals, waterfowl, beavers, songbirds. (We saw a bald eagle, elk, deer, pelicans, waterfowl, and beaver sign.)

Maps and Information: A free guide is available at the Colter Bay Visitor Center when it's open, from May through September. This map is helpful because of the maze of trails in this area.

The network of trails around Swan Lake in Grand Teton National Park is a great place for year-round exploration. This tangle of trails can give you a different look at a park known more for its high mountain treks.

67

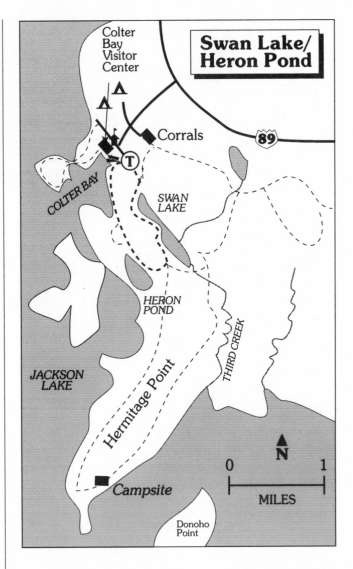

Swan Lake/
Heron Pond

Colter Bay Visitor Center

Corrals

89

COLTER BAY

SWAN LAKE

HERON POND

JACKSON LAKE

Hermitage Point

THIRD CREEK

Campsite

Donoho Point

0   N   1

MILES

The main attraction along these trails is the wildlife, especially as seen along Third Creek and around Swan Lake. If you go in the early morning or late evening, expect to see elk, moose, beavers, sandhill cranes, waterfowl, gulls, pelicans, or eagles.

The area features lodgepole pine forest, willow thickets, grassy meadows, and boggy wet areas. Swan Lake is loaded with lily pads that blossom in June and July. To the west across Jackson Lake is the dramatic backdrop of Grand Teton and Mount Moran.

The trails are very easy, and are great for children. Our kids were especially pleased with the red squirrels so intent on gathering pinecones for the coming winter that they often ran all around us, almost within touching distance. The network of trails in this area allows you to tailor a trip to your group's physical abilities. Don't miss the trail along Swan Lake. Here we spied several grazing elk. Moose are also very common in this area and along Third Creek.

For those wishing a longer trek, the trails out to Hermitage Point are just as easy, only longer. The view from the point across the lake and up the mountains is worth the trek (see Hike 31 on page 147).

There are opportunities for fishing along Jackson Lake, Heron Pond, or Third Creek. These waters contain mostly cutthroat trout.

These trails are also good for skiing and winter exploring. Skiers may have to park off the road near the entrance to the Colter Bay Visitor Center.

These trails are popular with horseback riders. Corrals access the system about 1.5 miles northeast of Swan Lake, off the road coming into the Colter Bay Visitor Center. On the down side, this usually means horse manure and extra flies.

Final Thoughts

The Colter Bay Visitor Center and Indian Arts Museum is well worth checking into. The center has books for sale, audiovisual presentations, an American Indian art collection, and other information and activities. Museum tours are offered daily. The center is open from May to October. There are also ranger-guided tours of Heron Pond and Swan Lake. Check at the visitor center for schedules.

Kid Comments
. . . .
Did you see how close that squirrel got to me?

It seems like the elk disappear and reappear along the lake.

Water lilies cover large portions of Heron Pond in the summer.

Short Hikes and Half-Day Hikes

In this chapter, families can expect to find walks that are mostly easy but that take more time than an hour and less than six hours. Some of these hikes can be appropriate for toddlers and preschoolers who are used to hiking.

Christian Pond/ Emma Matilda Lake

14

Main Attractions: Nice scenic views of Jackson and Emma Matilda lakes, and wildlife-viewing

Getting There: Drive 4 miles west of the Moran Junction to Jackson Lake Lodge. Park in the lot near the horse-rental corrals. The trail begins near the corrals and goes under the bridge toward Christian Pond.

Trail Distance: It's 2 miles to a nice overlook above the north side of the lake, 8 miles to loop completely around the lake

Elevation Gain/Loss: The trail gains 300 feet on the north side and flattens out around the south side

How Strenuous: Moderate. Toddlers and preschool children will do fine around Christian Pond. Hiking beyond the pond is not recommended for the younger set.

When to Go: Late May to October. Avoid this area after hunting season opens in October.

Animals to Watch For: Elk, moose, deer, beavers, songbirds, waterfowl (especially swans), squirrels

Emma Matilda Lake is a beautiful cresent-shaped lake more than three miles long and only accessible by backcountry trails. The trails around the pond and lake offer hikes for every skill level, with good opportunities for scenic views and wildlife-viewing.

Because of the nearby horse rentals at Jackson Lake Lodge, traffic can occasionally be heavy along some paths around the pond and lake, and horse manure on the trail can be a problem. But the trail along the northern part of the lake is not as heavily used, especially after the fork heading to Two Ocean Lake. Most people head over to Two Ocean Lake or stick to the trail along the south part of Emma Matilda Lake.

For families looking for a short hike with a very nice overall view of the Tetons, Jackson Lake, and Emma Matilda Lake, follow the trail around Christian Pond then take the fork to the north side of the lake. This trail soon begins to rise at a steady slope, and there are a few abrupt climbs. After two miles and about a three-hundred-foot gain, you reach a ridge above the lake and a marvelous view of Emma Matilda below and Jackson Lake in the distance. This ridge is prime elk habitat. Small herds of a dozen or more are often spotted in this area between Emma Matilda Lake and Two Ocean Lake.

If your group still has energy to burn, you can make the loop around the lake. The rest of the trail is downhill or flat hiking and takes you closer to the lake's shore. The trail circles around the east end of the lake and returns to Christian Pond.

If you are looking for an even

Bison are enormous. They can weigh up to 2,000 pounds and stand 6 feet at the shoulder. Bison are sometimes called buffalo, but true buffalo live only in Asia and Africa.

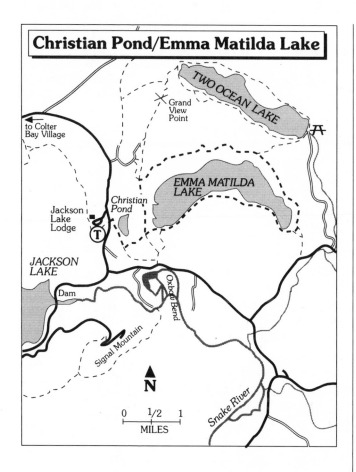

Christian Pond/Emma Matilda Lake

TWO OCEAN LAKE

Grand
View
Point

to Colter
Bay Village

EMMA MATILDA
LAKE

Christian
Pond

Jackson
Lake
Lodge

T

JACKSON
LAKE

Dam

Oxbow Bend

Signal Mountain

N

Snake River

0   1/2   1
MILES

more leisurely hike, skip the northern route and head along the southern trail. This trail takes you close to the lakeshore. Keep an eye out for moose along the edge of the lake, especially in early-morning and late-evening hours. The trail around Emma Matilda Lake is heavily wooded, making it a nice trail on which to hide from the hot summer sun. But come prepared with mosquito repellent.

This lake, like Two Ocean Lake, was formed by glaciers that gouged out the area during the last ice age.

The trail around Emma Matilda Lake is mostly easy and offers nice views of the lake.

When the glaciers retreated, the holes filled up with water to form the two lakes.

Emma Matilda Lake is named after the wife of William O. Owen. Owen, a resident of the valley in the late 1800s, was a topographer for the General Land Office. He and Emma attempted an unsuccessful climb up the Grand Teton in 1891. In 1898, Owen climbed the peak with Bishop Spalding, John Shive and Frank Petersen. Owen is often given credit as the first person to successfully climb the mountain.

Christian Pond is named after Charles A. Christian. Christian was the innkeeper of the original Jackson Lake Lodge at Moran.

Final Thoughts

Remember that Christian Pond is closed to fishing because the area is used by nesting swans.

Kid Comments

This is a pretty lake. Let's hike all the way around it.

15 South Darby Canyon Wind Cave

Main Attractions: Waterfalls, wildflowers, wildlife, and a fascinating wind cave

Getting There: From Victor, Idaho, drive 5.5 miles north on Highway 33. Turn right (east) onto a paved road. Look for signs at the beginning of the road for Darby Girls Camp. After a mile the road becomes gravel. After another .5-mile the road forks. Go right and follow this road about 6 miles to its end, where you may park.

Trail Distance: 3.4 miles one way

Elevation Gain/Loss: 1,800 feet up and back

How Strenuous: Mostly strenuous, but a well-made trail. Not recommended for toddlers and preschool children.

When to Go: Mid-June to October.

Animals to Watch For: Deer, elk, moose, small mammals, songbirds, and bighorn sheep

This is a fun trail with a super destination. The wind cave at the end of the trail adds an extra bit of fascination to an interesting hike with nice waterfalls and scenery. Sometimes the locals refer to this as the "Monument Trail" because of a cement and rock monument placed in the upper basin, near the wind cave. The monument is in remembrance of five people who died here after being struck by lightning during a thunderstorm. The group consisted of hikers from the nearby summer girls camp.

The trail starts off with a footbridge across Darby Creek, then begins to climb away from the creek. After about a half-mile the trail enters the Jedediah Smith Wilderness and crosses the South Fork of Darby Creek.

Be alert for wildlife in this creek area. On our hike we spotted a porcupine on the trail near the creek. My experience with these funny-looking critters is that they are often found near creeks or wet areas.

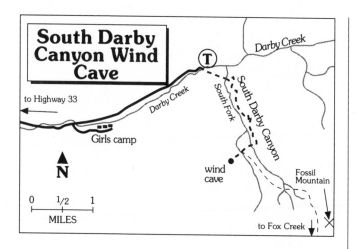

After crossing the creek, the trail climbs sharply up the canyon. Most of the tough part of the trail comes in the next 1.5 miles. The last mile climbs at a less-drastic slope.

An interesting phenomenon is that the creek disappears underground for a short way about a mile up the canyon. When the trail becomes easier, remember to look down into the canyon to see if the creek is still there. In late summer, the creek is often dry until you reach the mouth of the cave.

The trail continues to climb with a few switchbacks until it is near the canyon rim and into some less-forested terrain. Along this point watch the opposite rim for waterfalls. Late in the summer these can be somewhat diminished or nonexistent. As the trail approaches the upper basin, it enters a thickly forested area and turns west. Before entering the trees you should be able to see the wind cave along the western wall of the canyon. During wet years and early in the season there is a substantial flow of water coming from the mouth of the cave and cascading down the canyon.

In the meadows near the cave are fantastic wildflower displays during midsummer.

The entrance to the wind cave high in South Darby Canyon.

The trail forks just before you arrive at the monument. The fork heading up the basin along the creek is not shown on some maps. This unmaintained, and in some places nonexistent, trail climbs over the basin ridge and hooks up with the Fox Creek trail. The rocky ridges along the top edges of the canyon are good places to look for the very elusive bighorn sheep.

Continue on to the monument. The large marker serves as a good reminder of Mother Nature's fury. In discussing the tragedy with children, it's a good opportunity to teach them what to do during a thunderstorm in the mountains (see page 6).

From the monument, it's a steep scramble up switchbacks to the mouth of the wind cave. In wetter, cooler years, snow often lingers around the cave, making a climb up ill-advised. Make sure you bring along flashlights to enjoy some of the interior. On a hot day the gusts of wind through the cave are like a natural air conditioner. This cave is really a natural tunnel with wind pouring through from inlets farther up the canyon. The cave goes deep into the mountain and comes out at about the same level along the ridge about .75-mile up the canyon. But in between the entrance and exit are some forty-foot drops and climbs that require ropes, ice axes, crampons, and technical expertise to negotiate.

Because of the steepness of this hike, going back down can take less than half the time of going up. Don't let children go too fast, or nasty falls or sprains may be the result.

Final Thoughts

Although most trails are traveled least during the morning hours, this trail is an exception during the week. Groups from the nearby girls camp usually hike this trail in the morning and come back before dinner. To avoid weekday crowds, go in the evening. On weekends, go in the early morning.

Kid Comments
. . . .
I'm glad I brought this flashlight. It's dark in here!

16 Grand View Point

Main Attractions: One of the best scenic views of the upper valley, mountains, and Jackson Lake.

Getting There: Drive 1 mile north of Jackson Lake Lodge on Highway 89. Turn right (east) onto an unmarked dirt road. After about 200 yards, the road forks. Stay on the road to your right and drive to the end. Make sure to stick to the main dirt road—side roads dead-end. This road is okay for the family sedan, just take it slow and avoid the potholes and rocks. The last hundred yards of the road climb steeply just before the parking area. After a rainstorm this road may become impassable to most cars.

Trail Distance: 1.1 miles to the top of the viewpoint

Elevation Gain/Loss: 400 feet

How Strenuous: Strenuous, but short. You may have to carry toddlers most of the way up; preschoolers used to hiking should do okay, but give them time to rest.

When to Go: Mid- to late-May, depending on the snowmelt. The access road may be impassable after a heavy rain or snow.

Animals to Watch For: Elk, deer, moose, eagles, squirrels, songbirds, woodpeckers, bear

This is a short but tough hike with a great payoff at the top. Don't forget your camera or binoculars.

The hike is only 1.1 miles, but it's all uphill. The trail gains four hundred feet on its way to some of the best views of the northern half of the park.

To get to the trailhead, take a bumpy dirt road just past the Jackson Lake Lodge. There are no signs to help you out, so bring a map.

The hike begins to climb through a forest of spruce, Douglas fir, and lodgepole pine. Some of the old fir

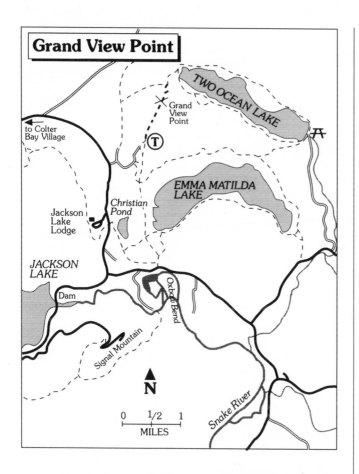

Grand View Point

Two Ocean Lake

Grand View Point

to Colter Bay Village

(T)

EMMA MATILDA LAKE

Christian Pond

Jackson Lake Lodge

JACKSON LAKE

Dam

Oxbow Bend

Signal Mountain

N

Snake River

0   1/2   1

MILES

trees in this area are huge; many are dead snags pocked with woodpecker holes. Have the children examine a few of the holes up close. Woodpeckers bore holes in the bark in search of insects. The *rat-a-tat-tat* of woodpeckers can occasionally be heard during hikes in the Tetons. With a sharp eye you can sometimes spot a nesting woodpecker. These birds build their temporary homes high in hollowed-out sections of trees. The hole or entrance to the nest is about the size of a fifty-cent piece. If the mom woodpecker has young inside, she will be flying constantly in and out of the hole with tasty bugs. Look for nesting woodpeckers in spring or early summer.

After about .75-mile up the trail, nice views will open up to the west side of the valley and also to the east side. When you are looking west, you'll see the Teton Range, with Jackson Lake spread out below. To the east, look for parts of Emma Matilda and Two Ocean lakes directly below you, and the Gros Ventre Range to the southeast. These views are an appetizer for what's to come.

As you continue up the hill, bald areas present themselves for good viewing opportunities. Eventually, just past a mile up the trail, the path reaches its highest point. This is a bald top offering a great 360-degree view. This is a nice place to linger for a snack. If you pushed and hauled little ones up to the top, it's a good idea to praise their efforts here.

Keep this hike in mind if you are visiting the area in the fall—late August and September. This side of the valley offers nice views of aspen groves and cottonwood trees that cluster along the Snake River. In autumn, these trees become a feast for the eyes in various shades of gold, yellow, and scarlet.

From the top of Grand View Point, you can return back to your vehicle the way you came, or, depending on your group's stamina, continue on the Two Ocean Lake trail. One possibility is to have one of the adults in your group hike back down to your car and drive around to the picnic area at Two Ocean Lake and meet up with the rest of the group, who hiked around the lake.

The trail down to Two Ocean Lake switchbacks down to the level of the lake and is then flat the rest of the way. It's easy hiking except for the distance, which is about five miles.

Final Thoughts

This area is open to hunters in October. Fall hikers should head to the western side of the park to avoid any hunting-associated hazards. Also, watch for bear around Emma Matilda and Two Ocean lakes.

KidComments
....

I'd like to go out to that big island in the middle of Jackson Lake someday.

Jenny Lake/Hidden Falls/Inspiration Point

Main Attractions: Scenic trail next to the mountains and along a gorgeous lake; wildlife-viewing; waterfalls; wonderful valley overlook; fishing; easy hiking; and lots of wild berries

Getting There: From the Moose Visitor Center, drive 7 miles north on the Teton Park Road to the South Jenny Lake Junction. Park near the Jenny Lake Visitor Center.

Trail Distance: From the East Shore boat dock to Hidden Falls is 2.5 miles; add .4-mile more to Inspiration Point; subtract 2 miles if you take the shuttle boat across the lake. The trail that circles Jenny Lake is 6.6 miles long.

Elevation Gain/Loss: The trail to Hidden Falls gains about 150 feet; the trail up to Inspiration Point gains another 267 feet; the trail around the lake gains about 100 feet

How Strenuous: Except for Inspiration Point, these hikes are mostly easy. Inspiration Point is not quite strenuous—it gains its elevation quickly but is only .4-mile up. If you have toddlers or small pre-schoolers you may want to take the shuttle-boat ride and just visit Hidden Falls.

When to Go: June to October. It's best to go early in the morning.

Animals to Watch For: Moose, deer, and small mammals

Maps and Information: Maps of the lake trails are available at the trailhead and at the Jenny Lake Visitor Center

This has got to be the most heavily hiked area in the entire Tetons. There are times when the trail will remind you of Grand Central Station. But despite the traffic, the scenery is stunning and worth the trip.

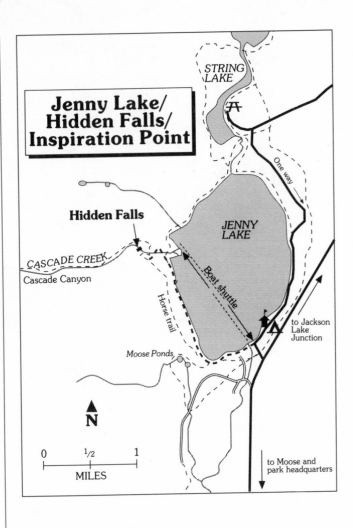

Jenny Lake/ Hidden Falls/ Inspiration Point

STRING LAKE

One way

Hidden Falls

JENNY LAKE

CASCADE CREEK

Cascade Canyon

Boat shuttle

Horse trail

to Jackson Lake Junction

Moose Ponds

N

to Moose and park headquarters

0   1/2   1
MILES

The most popular hiking route to Hidden Falls is to leave from the boat dock and hike around the south side of the lake. This route follows near the shoreline in several places and offers a nice view of the lake. The trail is mostly flat for the first .75-mile, then it climbs about fifty feet to an overlook of Moose Ponds. Beyond the ponds the trail enters lush, dense forest. Huckleberries grow in abundance throughout the

Hidden Falls and Inspiration Point area. They usually ripen in mid- to late summer.

At the two-mile mark, signs point the way to Hidden Falls. At the falls there are benches for sitting and taking in the view. The falls was a favorite spot for early settlers to the valley. It was named Hidden Falls because it couldn't be seen from the road on the east side of Jenny Lake. Jenny Lake was named by geologist Ferdinand Hayden, who surveyed the region in the 1870s, after the Shoshoni wife of his guide, Beaver Dick Leigh. Jenny and her six children died of smallpox in 1876.

The hike to Hidden Falls from String Lake is often less crowded and seems shorter. The trail is heavily wooded and also offers some very nice views of the lake.

From Hidden Falls it is a steep and rocky .4-mile up to Inspiration Point. The trail switchbacks up about 260 feet. If you don't rush it, you'll find it's not that tough a walk.

Inspiration Point offers a wonderful panoramic view of Jackson Hole. On clear days you will get a nice view of the Gros Ventre Range to the east.

The ground squirrels are very friendly in the area of Inspiration Point. Tell your children not to feed the animals, even if they see others doing so. Feeding these animals often leads to their poor health and dependence on handouts.

If your family has the energy to take the long way back from Hidden Falls, you can return to the parking area by following the trail around the north side of the lake. This trail is a mile longer than is returning back the way you came. It is also not as crowded as the other route.

If you wish to take an easy way to Hidden Falls and Inspiration Point, you can ride the shuttle boat across the lake. This route cuts two miles off the hike each way. A fee is charged for the ride, and you can cut the price by taking the shuttle one way rather than as a round-trip.

Kid Comments

· · · · · · · · · · · · ·

The squirrels sure are friendly here.

This is the prettiest waterfall I've ever seen.

Park visitors view Hidden Falls, on the west side of Jenny Lake.

Final Thoughts

There are times you can avoid the usual crowd of people and have the entire trail to yourself. Perhaps half the people who visit Hidden Falls and Inspiration Point do so via the shuttle boat. The boat typically stops running after the dinner hour, so if your group starts hiking when the last boat leaves the dock, by the time you arrive at Hidden Falls, very few people will be there. I have hiked from the forks of Cascade Canyon back to the Jenny Lake parking lot and passed only one person in the entire 6.5 miles because it was evening. If you go in the evening, leave yourself enough daylight for the return trip.

The best strategy may be to be on the trail when most visitors are still having breakfast. Early risers beat the heat and the crowds.

18 Leigh Lake

Main Attractions: Easy hiking, swimming, fishing, berry-picking, and wildlife-viewing

Getting There: Drive 14 miles north of Jackson on Highway 89 to Moose Junction. Turn left (west) and drive 11 miles to the North Jenny Lake Junction and turn left (west). Drive 2.5 miles to the String Lake picnic area and park at the third, northern-most parking area. The trailhead is at the north end of the picnic area.

Trail Distance: From the trailhead to the north end of Leigh Lake it's 3.7 miles

Elevation Gain/Loss: 30 feet up and down

How Strenuous: Easy. Toddlers and preschoolers will probably limit your distance along the lake, but even a short distance is enjoyable.

When to Go: Mid-May to October

Animals to Watch For: Some waterfowl, moose, elk, deer, squirrels, and songbirds

The trail along Leigh Lake is great for short hikes to see some of the scenery, or longer hikes to a fun beach area, or even an overnight trip.

The entire trail is flat and easy and parallels the east shore of the lake, usually just a few steps from the water. You find yourself constantly looking at the beautiful blues and greens of the lake with the world-class scenery of the Tetons in the background. The lake gets its green color from glacial meltwater off Mount Moran. The lake is 250 feet deep in the center.

This hike starts from the String Lake picnic area and travels along the east side of String Lake for .9-mile. At this point the trail forks. The left trail, going west, crosses the Leigh Lake outlet and circles around String Lake. Stick to the right trail, heading north.

As you walk along the lake, look for interesting tiny

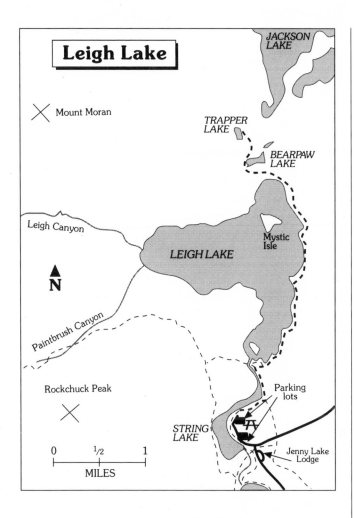

Leigh Lake

JACKSON LAKE

Mount Moran

TRAPPER LAKE

BEARPAW LAKE

Leigh Canyon

LEIGH LAKE

Mystic Isle

N

Paintbrush Canyon

Rockchuck Peak

Parking lots

STRING LAKE

Jenny Lake Lodge

0   ½   1

MILES

rock islands near the shore. Some of these islands have large lone trees that somehow manage to live with very little soil. The children should find these fascinating.

Tell the family to listen for the chatter of red squirrels on this trail. As you pass each squirrel's territory, it begins to "cuss out" intruders with shrill chirps. Also look for signs of moose along the trail. Hikers who come early in the morning or around dusk may even spot the gigantic creatures. Their tracks resemble that of a deer but are four times larger. The prints are often more than six inches long. Other tell-tale signs include dark brown or black droppings about two inches long that look like monster gel-caps.

Our children will always remember the "stick" that Dad stepped over on this trail and that suddenly came to life and slithered across our twelve-year-old's foot. We managed to block this harmless snake's escape route long enough for a quick photo session. Then it escaped for good.

Probably the best part of the Leigh Lake hike is the views of 12,605-foot Mount Moran. Mount Moran is the peak to the northwest of the lake. Directly west of the lake are two large canyons, Paintbrush Canyon (the one on the south) and Leigh Canyon. North of Leigh Canyon is Mount Moran. The huge white patch just below the top is Falling Ice Glacier. This glacier is one of several that have lived on Mount Moran for centuries. Each year, the glacier grows during the winter and shrinks during the summer, sending huge chunks of ice down the mountainside to the valley below. On the north side of the mountain are three larger glaciers. Mount Moran has five of the park's twelve active glaciers. Also, look for the "dike," a 150-foot-wide strip of black rock that cuts vertically through the face of Mount Moran. Molten magma filled a crack in the older rock to form this huge strip. This dike extends from near the west shore of Leigh Lake all the way to Idaho, about seven miles to the west.

After about 2.3 miles, you come to a sandy beach on the lakeshore. This is a great place to splash and wade in the water. A sandy beach is a bit of a novelty in the Tetons—most of the area's lakes have rocky shores.

This is a good place to turn around if your little ones are sending fatigue signals. If your clan still has the energy, you can continue on another 1.5 miles to the end of the trail at Trapper Lake and Bearpaw Lake. These are popular backcountry camping sites and good bets for family backpackers because of the beautiful area and the easy hiking.

Kid Comments
. . . .
I'd like to come back and camp out.
Can we?

Short Hikes and Half-Day Hikes

Mount Moran dominates the skyline along the Leigh Lake Trail.

Leigh Lake also offers fair fishing for Mackinaw and cutthroat trout. If you're very serious about catching fish, though, a canoe is probably your best bet here.

Be sure to look for wild huckleberries if you are hiking this trail in late summer. These berries are a delicious snack for hikers as well as an important, high-calorie food for wildlife. The bluish purple berries, about the size of a pea, grow on waist-high bushes. Whortle-berries also grow in this area. The whortleberry bush is low to the ground—less than a foot high—with tiny round leaves. Look for the tiny red berries.

Final Thoughts

Remember that mosquitoes can be thick around Leigh Lake, especially in June. To help make your hike a success, bring along insect repellent, long-sleeve shirts, pants, or even a head net.

Phelps Lake Overlook

Main Attractions: Scenic views, cascading water, and wildlife viewing

Getting There: The trailhead is off the Moose-Wilson Road 3 miles south of Moose. Drive 3 miles southwest on the Moose-Wilson Road from Moose and turn right (west) at the Death Canyon trailhead sign on a narrow paved road. After a half-mile the road becomes a bumpy dirt road for another half-mile. There are a few overflow parking areas before you get to the trailhead.

Trail Distance: .9-mile up to Phelps Lake Overlook

Elevation Gain/Loss: 400 feet up to Phelps Lake Overlook

How Strenuous: Moderately tough hiking up to Phelps Lake Overlook. Toddlers and preschoolers accustomed to walking should enjoy the trip up to the overlook, but going beyond the overlook is not recommended for toddlers and preschoolers.

When to Go: After the snows are gone in late May or mid-June to October

Animals to Watch For: Lots of marmots, squirrels, moose, songbirds, and pikas

The short hike up to Phelps Lake Overlook climaxes with a terrific view of the park's fourth-largest lake. The trail takes you through stands of lodgepole pine and across footbridges that span several small streams. This is a wet area, especially in the early spring. Because of all the water, you'll find thick vegetation here that is not found in other parts of the Tetons.

The trail soon leaves the woods and enters a meadow area. This area is fringed with aspens and scrubs. It is also painted with the color of a variety of

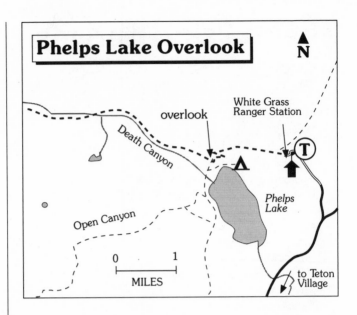

Phelps Lake Overlook

N

White Grass
Ranger Station

overlook

Death Canyon

T

Open Canyon

Phelps
Lake

0   1

MILES

to Teton
Village

wildflowers. Occasionally you will pass by some massive Douglas fir trees. We were impressed by one more than three feet wide that forked about thirty feet up. On our hike up we met a three-foot-long snake that was crossing the trail.

The trail is mostly a gradual incline until just before the overlook, when it climbs more steeply. When you come to the overlook, stop awhile, sit on one of the large rocks, and soak in the view.

Phelps Lake is about 1.5 miles long and more than 150 feet deep. On the far side of the lake you can see several buildings. This is the JY Ranch. The ranch was originally established by Louis H. Joy in 1908 as one of the first dude ranches in Jackson Hole. It is now owned by the Rockefeller family.

The lake was named by F. V. Hayden, one of the area's first government surveyors, after a trapper named Phelps. His full name is unknown. Historians believe Phillips Canyon and Phillips Pass are named after the

Phelps Lake Overlook offers a quiet place to enjoy a beautiful view.

same trapper, whose name was misspelled in the diary of Beaver Dick Leigh.

From the overlook, the trail switchbacks down about four hundred feet to near the lake, where it forks. The trail heading south, the Valley Trail, goes around the west side of the lake. The trail to the right heads up Death Canyon and along its creek.

This trail is often traveled by moose heading up to the lush upper canyon or down to Phelps Lake.

Final Thoughts

This is a popular trail. To avoid most of the crowds, go during the week and start early in the morning. Also, take plenty of water if you plan on hiking beyond the overlook.

Ski Lake Trail

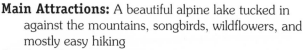

Main Attractions: A beautiful alpine lake tucked in against the mountains, songbirds, wildflowers, and mostly easy hiking

Getting There: From Wilson, Wyoming, drive 4.5 miles west on Highway 22 toward Teton Pass. Watch for the sign for Phillips Canyon. Pull off the road there and into a parking area on the left (south) side. From the parking area, walk across the highway and up the jeep road for about .3-mile. The sign for the trailhead is on the left.

Trail Distance: 4.6 miles round-trip from the parking area

Elevation Gain/Loss: 850 feet up and down

How Strenuous: Almost easy, not quite moderate. With rests and patience, your preschoolers should make it all the way; not recommended for toddlers.

When to Go: Late June to October

Animals to Watch For: Deer, elk, moose, songbirds, eagles, small mammals, and waterfowl at the lake

This trail surprised us in that we were expecting a tougher hike. The hardest part of the hike seemed to be fighting off the occasional black fly. With a few exceptions, the elevation gain is spread out pretty evenly across the two miles of trail.

This is a popular trail, and it is not unusual to see more than a half-dozen cars in the parking area off the highway.

You start off by hiking up the jeep trail about .3-mile. The trail goes through several open areas that feature an abundance of wildflowers in midsummer. The forest is mostly lodgepole pine, with some spruce and fir mixed in.

At the one-mile mark, the trail forks at a large flat

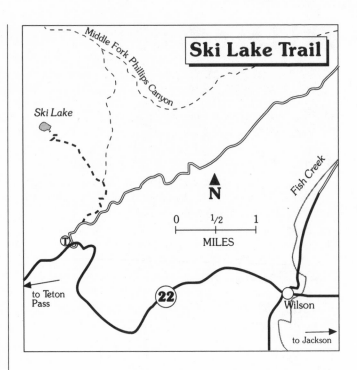

Ski Lake Trail

Middle Fork Phillips Canyon

Ski Lake

Fish Creek

N

0   1/2   1
MILES

to Teton Pass

22

Wilson

to Jackson

meadow that is about the size of a couple of football fields. Early in the summer this meadow has a small stream passing through it. The stream is usually gone by midsummer. The right fork heads up to Phillips Pass, which is another three miles up. Even though this trail climbs to the crest of the Tetons, most of the hiking is moderate. Much of this is due to the fact that the trailhead starts out at such a high elevation. This is a popular starting point for hikers connecting with the Teton Crest Trail—a trail which traverses the length of the mountain range.

The left fork trail continues on to Ski Lake. In a few hundred yards this trail comes to another stream which often has a good flow until late summer. The stream is only a few feet wide and has nice stepping-stones for crossing. This nameless stream comes from a pond to the southwest of Ski Lake. A little distance past this

Ski Lake offers a beautiful alpine view after a short, almost-easy hike.

stream the trail begins its only serious climb. Remember to look back during one of your rest stops for a nice view of the Jackson Hole valley and the Gros Ventre Range beyond.

The trail soon follows the outlet stream of Ski Lake. During dry years, the shallow-outlet stream dries up by midsummer.

Ski Lake is a beautiful lake jewel about a dozen acres in area and tucked right up against the peaks. As you walk around it you will notice that its bottom quickly drops out of sight. The deepest part is up by the mountain. Another view of the lake can be obtained with a bit more effort by taking the side trail that climbs up the north side of the lake.

Ski Lake is often visited by waterfowl, mostly ducks.

Final Thoughts

The only negative I can think of for this hike was that we did encounter some black flies. Unlike mosquitoes, black flies take big painful bites when they attack. There are a few repellents that keep black flies somewhat at bay. Don't forget to bring them along on this hike.

Snake River Angler's Trail

Main Attractions: Excellent fishing along the Snake River; wildlife-viewing and easy hiking

Getting There: Drive 1.25 miles south of the Signal Mountain Lodge on the Teton Park Road. Turn left (east) on a dirt road and drive 3.75 miles to the end of the road to a parking area near the river.

Trail Distance: 2 to 4 miles round-trip, depending on how far up or down the river you want to go

Elevation Gain/Loss: Trail has only a few ups and downs of about 35 feet

How Strenuous: Easy. Recommended for preschoolers and older.

When to Go: Late May or early June, when the dirt road is dry. Avoid this area after hunting season has opened in October.

Animals to Watch For: Moose, elk, deer, waterfowl, songbirds, eagles, ospreys, beavers, and small mammals

This is a great place to avoid the crowds that flock to the mountain trails. It's also a wonderful place to observe wildlife such as moose, elk, and waterfowl. But most of all, this is a place to go fishing.

When you arrive at the end of the bumpy dirt road, you have two options: hike upstream or down. There are no formal maintained trails along the river, but you will find that the trails are well used by wildlife as much as by humankind. Either direction provides fine fishing opportunities and a close-up view of truly wild river country. The hiking is easy, but come prepared to wade the side channels. I suggest that, rather than outfit the entire family in costly waders, just go on a warm day and have everyone wear old tennis shoes.

If you are not into fishing, don't worry. This area

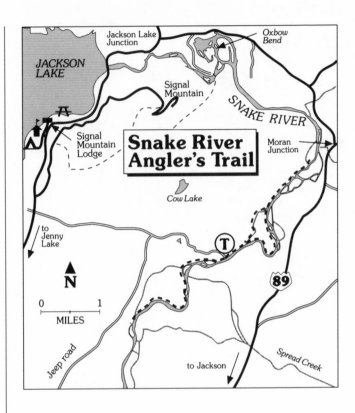

has superior wildlife-viewing opportunities, especially early or late in the day. Expect to see a variety of waterfowl, including swans, geese, cranes, ducks, and herons. You should see fresh moose, deer, and elk tracks. And if you aren't too noisy, you will probably see at least one member of the deer family. We saw an elk cow and calf on one of our upstream visits. There is also the work of beaver around many of the side channels and along the main river. It is sometimes amazing to see the size of trees felled by these large rodents. Songbirds, bald eagles, and ospreys are also in abundance in this area.

This is a beautiful area to visit in the fall because of the large stands of cottonwoods. There is also fir, spruce, pine, and aspen.

Let's look at the upstream route first. From the parking area, walk straight to the river, then follow the well-beaten path north along the river. About a half-mile upstream you will come to the first channel. This is a good place to try your luck for some of the river's famous cutthroat trout. Remember that trout tend to lie along eddy lines where fast-moving water meets slower-moving water. They also lie behind gravel bars, rocks, logs, and other obstructions. The side channels on the river also offer good fishing opportunities depending on how much water is flowing through them. Fish these channels as you'd fish a regular creek. Most side channels are dependent on the amount of water being released from the Jackson Lake Dam. Late in the year, many side channels are shallow or completely dried up.

The main channel of the river makes a giant hook about one-eighth of a mile past the first side channel. Continue to follow the river and you will come to more gravel bars and small islands. Avoid the temptation of trying to wade out to these islands unless the water is no deeper than your knees. The river claims many lives each year, mostly of boaters and rafters but occasionally of anglers who fall in the water and find the current swifter than they anticipated. I tell my children never to step into the river where it is higher than their knees.

If you haven't been beguiled into fishing a stretch of water yet, there is plenty of good water for the next two miles. If you hike more than a mile from the parking area you can feel confident that you are fishing water usually only seen by drift-boaters.

If you hike downstream from the parking area you will come to some nice side channels and islands after about a third of a mile.

Final Thoughts

The trails in this area are all informal. Because none are maintained, expect to be jumping the occasional deadfall and wading a side channel to get to certain areas. This can add to the adventure for many children.

Kid Comments
• • • • • • • • • • • •
Was this tree chopped down by a beaver? It's huge. How did it do that?

22 String Lake Trail

Main Attractions: Very nice scenic views, swimming, and wildlife-viewing

Getting There: Drive 14 miles north of Jackson on Highway 89 to Moose Junction. Turn left (west) and drive 11 miles to the North Jenny Lake Junction and turn left (west). Drive 2.5 miles to the String Lake picnic area and park at the first parking lot near the footbridge.

Trail Distance: 3.4 miles around

Elevation Gain/Loss: 200 feet up and down

How Strenuous: Mostly easy, with some upward stretches on the mountainside. Not recommended for toddlers or preschoolers who haven't done much walking.

When to Go: May to October.

Animals to Watch For: Marmots and other small mammals, eagles, ospreys, moose, elk, deer, songbirds, and waterfowl

String Lake is a great place to get wet. Families come to String Lake to splash and swim, canoe, or just float on inner tubes. The lake is shallow, only about ten feet at its deepest. It's a great place to relax at the picnic tables and soak up the view of the Tetons. But don't forget the trail that circles the lake.

The String Lake Trail features two fun footbridges across the lake's inlet and outlet. The hiking is mostly easy and offers nice views of the valley and nearby mountains.

Going clockwise from the trailhead around the lake plunges you into a dense lodgepole pine and Douglas fir forest. The trail soon forks; the left route takes you around Jenny Lake to Hidden Falls. Take the right fork and continue around String Lake. On the west side of the lake, the trail begins to climb and distance itself from the lake, giving hikers a nice view of the lake and valley.

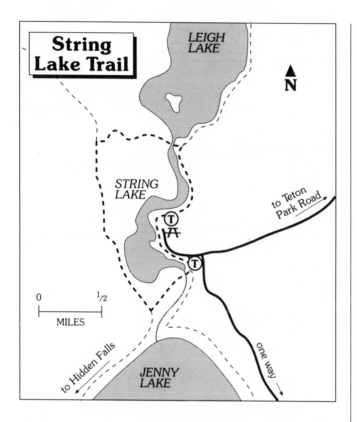

When the trail climbs sharply into a rocky, scrubby area about three-quarters of a mile from the outlet stream, keep a sharp lookout for marmots. These chubby little fellows, otherwise known as rockchucks, will usually perch on top of a rock and will occasionally whistle to one another until intruders scare them back into their burrows. If you spot one as you approach the rocky area, stop and remain still. They will often linger out in the open longer if you give them some distance. Pausing also allows your children the opportunity to see them. Marmots can be very friendly at times. I've had them follow me from rock to rock as I walked along the trail. But they vanish in the rocks as soon as you invade their comfort zone.

The bridge across the String Lake inlet gives children an extra bit of fun.

About a quarter-mile past the rocky area the trail passes an avalanche zone. Evidence of past snowslides down the slopes of 11,144-foot Rockchuck Peak will be obvious. Here, all the trees have been swept clean off the mountainside almost to the valley floor. The tremendous power of avalanches can be seen in the effects on the trees and rocks. Point out to children some of the large trees that have been uprooted or snapped in two and stripped of limbs. Fortunately for hikers, the danger of avalanche is long gone by late spring. Snow often covers this stretch of the trail into early summer. If snow is present, be careful with your footing as you cross.

The trail continues to climb until it comes to another fork. The left fork goes up Paintbrush Canyon, a very strenuous hike into the heart of the Tetons. Take the right fork. From here, the trail goes downhill to cross another footbridge over the Leigh Lake outlet or the String Lake inlet, depending on your point of view. Head left to pick up the Leigh Lake trail or right to return back to your vehicle and the picnic area.

Final Thoughts

There is an unmaintained trail heading north from the String Lake inlet bridge that leads to some nice backcountry campsites. This is a good trail for first-time backpackers and family backpackers looking for an easy overnight trip. The trail heads north along the west side of Leigh Lake. There are some nice sandy beaches and lots of woods to enjoy.

Kid Comments
• • • • • • • • • • • •
This is a pretty view of the lake from up here.

23 Taggart and Bradley Lakes

Main Attractions: Very nice scenic lake views, a cascading stream, fishing, wildflowers, and wildlife-viewing

Getting There: Drive 14 miles north from Jackson on Highway 89 to Moose Junction. Turn left (west) and drive north on the Teton Park Road 4 miles to the Taggart Lake trailhead parking lot, on the left (west) side of the the road.

Trail Distance: 1.6 miles straight up to Taggart Lake; 5.5 miles for the big loop along Beaver Creek and up to both lakes

Elevation Gain/Loss: 250 feet to 400 feet, depending on the route you choose

How Strenuous: Moderate. Not recommended for toddlers, but preschoolers used to walking can make it to Taggart Lake.

When to Go: Mid-May to October

Animals to Watch For: Moose, elk, deer, small mammals, songbirds, waterfowl, and eagles

This is a popular hike, and for good reason: the trail is not too difficult and takes you to some beautiful lakes at the base of the Tetons.

The Taggart Lake Trail gives visitors a good look at the effects of forest fire and how the forest renews itself. Generally after a fire, the vegetation that follows is more diverse than before and caters to a larger variety of wildlife. This trail gives adults an opportunity to show children the dramatic changes fire brings to the forest. The difference becomes more dramatic if hikers continue on to Bradley Lake, which was untouched by the fire.

In August of 1985, lightning touched off a forest fire that burned more than one thousand acres on the lake's southeast side. Firefighters fought the fire from

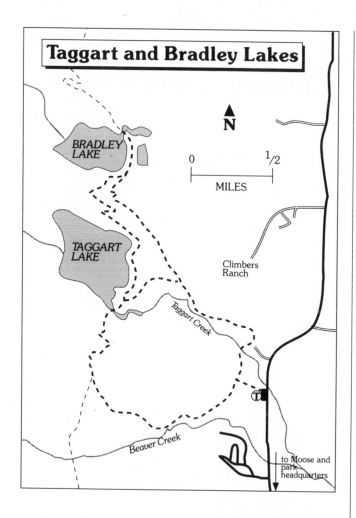

Taggart and Bradley Lakes

BRADLEY
LAKE

N

0   1/2

MILES

TAGGART
LAKE

Climbers
Ranch

Taggart Creek

T

Beaver Creek

to Moose and
park
headquarters

the beginning because it was close to the Beaver Creek residential area. But because it struck in August, the driest time of the year, it quickly went out of control. What eventually turned the tide against the fire was a change in the weather. Light rains and cooler temperatures helped put it out.

Everywhere you look are gray skeleton trees standing tall and lifeless. Below, on the forest floor, are small juvenile trees crowding in to take advantage of the lack of forest canopy. Many of the new trees are aspens. These small groves of aspens are often the first to take advantage of forest areas that are burned or knocked down by avalanches. In the autumn, the leaves of these trees turn a bright gold and orange. Wildflowers also proliferate in these open areas, especially in late spring and early summer. Listen for woodpeckers digging about the dead trees for insects. We could clearly hear a woodpecker's *rat-a-tat-tat* as we passed through the burned trees.

There are two routes up to the lakes from the trailhead. The trail leaves the parking lot and crosses a flat area. You'll notice a few ditches in this flat area. These were dug by a homesteader before the 1920s to water crops and cattle. At about the quarter-mile point the trail forks. The left trail follows Beaver Creek, and the right goes along the Taggart Lake outlet—Taggart Creek—up to the lake. Choose your path depending on your family's ability. The Taggart Lake route climbs 300 feet, while the Beaver Creek route climbs 350 feet and takes an extra half-mile to get to the lake. I like the Beaver Creek route because it avoids some of the extra traffic and makes for a nice loop hike if you are planning on going to both lakes.

The Beaver Creek Trail circles around the moraine that encloses Taggart Lake, then switches back up to the top of the moraine. Pause at the top of the hill for some first-class views. Also keep an eye out for circling eagles. We watched a pair of adult eagles being followed noisily by a juvenile. If you come this way from midsummer to late summer, watch for wild berries along the trail. At the top of the moraine you can try to picture how glaciers gouged out the bowl to form Taggart and Bradley lakes as they pushed down from the mountain canyon. Taggart Lake was named after W. Rush Taggart, the assistant geologist on the F. V. Hayden expedition that surveyed the region in 1872. Bradley Lake was named by Hayden for his chief geologist, Frank H. Bradley.

From here the trail winds down to Taggart Lake.

Kid Comments
....
I'd like to build a house and live right here.

Kids seem to be attracted to the bridge across the outlet of Taggart Lake.

Children will love to play on the large footbridge that crosses the lake's southern arm.

Taggart and Bradley lakes are open to swimming, and if you enjoy fishing, don't forget to bring your gear. The fishing in these lakes can be pretty fair. Expect cutthroat trout, brook trout, whitefish, chubs, and others.

Just after the bridge, the trail forks. The right trail leads back to the parking lot; the left heads around the lake and climbs another 120 feet up to Bradley Lake. As the trail leaves Taggart Lake, you soon enter the unburned area. This gives hikers an idea of what the forest used to look like before the fire raced through. After the trail reaches the lake, you can continue on another quarter-mile to another large footbridge over the northeast arm of the lake. Beyond the bridge the trail continues for another strenuous 4.4 miles to Amphitheater and Surprise lakes. Unless your group has energy to burn, I suggest you attack the Amphitheater trail from the Lupine Meadows trailhead. This approach trims about 1.5 miles.

From Bradley Lake, head back to the parking lot via the eastern route. After an initial climb out of the bowl that holds Bradley Lake, the trail steadily slopes down to Taggart Creek. Taggart Creek is an impressive cascade, boiling down the hillside.

Final Thoughts

Go early in the morning. There are two good reasons for going early. Most of this area is an old burn and offers little protection from the sun. Children, and adults, tend to wilt in the heat of the day, so hiking in the cool of the morning makes a lot of sense. Also, hiking in the morning avoids the crowds that usually start coming here about lunchtime.

Teton Pass Trail

Main Attractions: Scenic views, fields of wildflowers, and easy hiking

Getting There: From Jackson, Wyoming, drive 14 miles west on Highway 22 to Teton Pass. Pull off the highway into the parking area on the south side.

Trail Distance: 1 mile to wooded area; 2 miles to Black Canyon Trail

Elevation Gain/Loss: 200 feet up to the microwave station; another 200 feet to the wooded section about 1 mile from the trailhead

How Strenuous: Mostly easy, but you may find yourself short of breath because of the altitude (8,700 feet). Toddlers and preschoolers may only be able to go a short way, but this should be enough to see the nice view and many of the wildflowers.

When to Go: Before July, there may still be some snow on the trail

Animals to Watch For: Songbirds, small mammals, moose, and deer

The nice part about this hike is that your car does most of the work of climbing to the top of the mountains. After all that elevation gain in your car, the trail is mostly gentle in its ups and downs. The best time to visit this trail is midsummer, when all of the snow is gone.

The large treeless areas of this mountain are covered with a fantastic display of wildflowers, usually by mid-July depending on the year. Dozens of different varieties—blues, purples, whites, yellows, oranges, the whole crayon box—will dazzle the hiker. On warm days the flowers are buzzing with butterflies. Some children will settle on one flower as a favorite; others will keep changing their minds as a new variety is spotted.

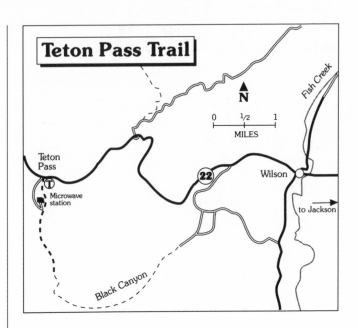

Teton Pass Trail

N

0   ½   1
MILES

Teton Pass

T

Microwave station

22

Wilson

Fish Creek

to Jackson

Black Canyon

Kid Comments

Too bad
Mom didn't
come with
us. She'd
love all
these
wildflowers.

After the flowers, the other nice feature is the view. From this trail's vantage point you can see several miles down into Jackson Hole. You can see the Snake River and the town of Wilson, with Fish Creek winding through it. The mountains directly east in the distance are the Gros Ventre Range.

The first one hundred yards of the trail climbs sharply, then levels off and enters the first section of wildflowers before entering a cluster of trees. The trail soon exits the trees and enters more fields of wildflowers. At about the .4-mile mark you will pass a microwave relay station and another building storing tools for avalanche rescue. Jackson Hole's main electrical power lines also pass through this area.

The treeless areas on the mountain were stripped mainly by the action of sliding snow. Nevertheless, the area is popular with skiers, both Nordic and alpine. The alpine skiers take the direct route down, and the Nordic skiers use the same trail hikers use in the summer.

At the one-mile mark the trail enters thick forest and switchbacks a few times up to the top of the ridge. This is where most people turn around and head back to the car. On a hot day this forested area feels as much as ten to fifteen degrees cooler.

From here the trail continues to climb to 9,200 feet, then drops down Black Canyon for about three miles, where it enters the summer-home area at Wilson. If you are interested in taking this trail all the way, understand that although the hiking is downhill and fairly easy, you will need a shuttle vehicle to get back up to the top of Teton Pass. Also, be aware that this trail is popular with mountain bikers.

Final Thoughts

Just to play it safe, it is a good idea to hold younger children's hands through the parts of the trail that pass over very steep sloping areas.

25 | Two Ocean Lake

Main Attractions: Scenic lake views, fishing, wildlife-viewing, few crowds

Getting There: Drive 1 mile north of Moran Junction and turn right (east) on the Pacific Creek Road. Drive about 1.3 miles and turn left (north) on Two Ocean Road, which is gravel. Drive 2 miles to the end of this road and park at a picnic area. This road may be impassable after heavy rain or snow.

Trail Distance: 3 miles from trailhead to the west end of the lake; 6 miles completely around

Elevation Gain/Loss: 30 feet

How Strenuous: Easy to moderate, depending on how far you go. The entire trail around the lake is not recommended for toddlers and preschoolers.

When to Go: May through September. Avoid this area during hunting season.

Animals to Watch For: Elk, moose, deer, waterfowl, eagles, bears, and small mammals. Beaver activity is apparent.

Two Ocean Lake offers a variety of activities with one additional feature you may find most appealing: fewer crowds. Because this area is reached by a dirt road, it gets relatively few visitors.

Two Ocean Lake features hiking, fishing, canoeing, and wildlife-viewing. The trail around the lake is flat and great for beginners. If you go in late June to mid-July, expect to see a wonderful display of wildflowers in the meadows around the lake. There are a few picnic tables and toilets at the trailhead.

Two Ocean Lake gets its name from being near the Continental Divide, where some streams flow west to the Pacific Ocean and others flow east, eventually arriving at the Atlantic Ocean. Two Ocean Lake drains into Pacific Creek. Two Ocean Lake and its twin, Emma

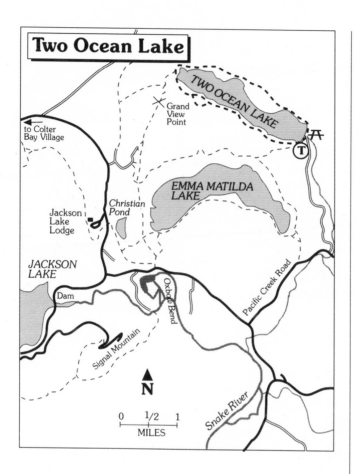

Matilda Lake, were formed by glaciers that left deep gouges that eventually became the lakes.

The trail around Two Ocean Lake is about seven miles long. If you are not sure your group can make the entire trip, start the hike on the east side by crossing the footbridge over the lake's outlet. The east-side trail takes you through more meadows. As you cross the footbridge, look down the outlet creek for beaver dams.

This hike goes through some nice aspen groves. These are often called "quaking aspens," because the leaves make a lot of noise when the wind blows. Aspens

Two Ocean Lake features hiking in the less-visited eastern side of Grand Teton National Park.

offer a different look to the area in the fall—late August and September. The leaves turn a beautiful gold and orange color against the solid green of the pines and fir trees. A fun thing to point out to the kids are the scars and scabs on the small aspen trees. If you look long enough you will see fresh brown scars that are caused by elk and deer polishing their antlers on the bark of the trees. It seems that aspen are the favorite scratching post of these animals. Sometimes the elk and deer pick on one small aspen tree and eventually kill it. The dark scabs on large aspens are caused by elk feeding on the bark during the wintertime. The Two Ocean Lake area has a good deal of resident elk. Your best chance of spotting them is to hike early in the morning or after dinner.

The lake also attracts a variety of waterfowl. Ducks, geese, and sandhill cranes have all been spotted here. After little more than a mile, the trail crosses a large meadow and creek. Willow brush, a mainstay of beaver diet, clogs the mouth of the stream. Look along the shore for a beaver lodge and other beaver-built features. These stream areas are also a favorite haunt of moose, deer, and elk. At the western end of the lake, three miles from the picnic area, are some old beaver dams.

Two Ocean Lake offers some fishing opportunities. Although it's hard to predict where they'll be biting, a good place to try your luck would be around the stream inlets on the north side. The water around the picnic area is weedy and yields mostly chubs.

Final Thoughts

Swimming is not recommended at Two Ocean Lake because of the large number of cold-water leeches it contains. Also, don't forget to bring a good supply of mosquito repellent for this area.

Kid Comments

Are there fish in this lake? Let's try and catch one.

Mule deer get their names from their extra large ears that move constantly and independently, listening for danger. They stand about 3.5 feet at the shoulder and have a white rump patch and a black-tipped tail. When they sense danger, they often leap stiff-legged, with all four feet off the ground.

All-Day and Overnight Hikes

This group of trails take families farther into the backcountry. The trips are usually more strenuous because of the extra length and elevation gain. These hikes are usually not appropriate for toddlers or preschoolers unless they can be carried easily in child carriers. The hikes usually last more than five hours.

These trails are not for beginners, but rather offer something for families to work up to. Many of these trails can offer unforgettable experiences.

The trails suggested as possible overnight hikes are mainly introductory. For more information on backpacking as a family activity, refer to So, You Want to Go Backpacking, on page 183.

Alaska Basin

26

Main Attractions: Wildflowers, wildlife, beautiful scenery, subalpine meadows, gorgeous alpine lakes, and granite outcrops

Getting There: From Victor, Idaho, drive 8 miles north on Highway 33 to Driggs. Turn right (east) at the main intersection, and follow the signs to Grand Targhee Ski Resort; drive 6 miles and turn right onto a dirt road with a sign for Teton Campground. Drive 5 miles to the trailhead/parking lot for South Teton Creek Trail.

Trail Distance: 8 miles one way to the basin lakes; another 2.5 miles up to the top of Hurricane Pass

Elevation Gain/Loss: 2,400 feet from the trailhead up to basin lakes

How Strenuous: Moderate for the first 4 miles, strenuous the last 3 miles. The hike to Sunset Lake and up to Hurricane Pass is a real workout; only the first few miles are recommended for toddlers to preschool age.

When to Go: Late June or early July to late September. The trail is still snowed in through May.

Animals to Watch For: Moose, deer, songbirds, marmots, pikas, porcupine, and other small mammals; bighorn sheep are often seen along the rocky ridges

This is one of the most popular backpacking and horseback-riding trails on the western side of the Tetons, next to the Table Mountain Trail. What makes this trail so popular is its magical beauty from the lower parts of the canyon all the way to the captivating basin lakes.

Although the trail does gain almost twenty-five hundred feet, most of the gain is gradual and spread out over eight miles. There are also good footbridges over the creeks.

From the trailhead, the path immediately enters the Jedediah Smith Wilderness. The most striking features in the first few miles are the wonderful wildflowers and the lively creek, which has some stretches where it cascades and drops.

At about the fourth mile, the trail forks. The trail to the right heads up Devils Stairs. This is a very strenuous route of switchbacks and narrow paths—I don't recommend it for young children.

The last half of the canyon is heavily forested with lodgepole pine, fir, and spruce. On our backpacking trip, we crossed paths with four different porcupines during the twilight hours before crawling into our sleeping bags. We were also awakened by a curious porcupine checking out our camp in the middle of the night. There is a nice but well-used campsite around mile seven. This is a popular area with outfitters using horses.

A good strategy for those who don't want to haul a full pack all the way to the top and back is to look for a campsite after the first four and a half to five miles, then stash your overnight gear and hike to the lakes and up to Hurricane Pass if you have the energy.

At about 7.5 miles, the trail switchbacks over a ridge and into Alaska Basin. Historians believe this beautiful rocky basin was named by settlers who returned from an Alaskan gold rush. The Basin Lakes are real gems and definitely worth the long hike. The basin area has special regulations to help protect its fragile alpine terrain. No camping with stock animals or stock grazing is allowed, and campfires are forbidden.

One fun thing you'll notice right away about Alaska Basin is its marmots. They seem to have no fear of people. As we hiked along the trail, we had several marmot escorts trotting along the rocks and boulders beside us.

Kid Comments

Is that ice floating out in the middle of the lake?

A few miles from Alaska Basin is Hurricane Pass. From the top of the pass, hikers can look down on Schoolroom Glacier with the Grand Teton to the east.

Some of the lakes may still have large chunks of ice floating in the center, even in mid- to late July. One of the prettier lakes is Mirror Lake, on the south side of the basin.

Be careful about heading off on some of the other trails, such as up to Mount Meek Pass or over the Hurricane Pass. Any direction you go, count on some strenuous hiking. The trip north to Sunset Lake is a tough .6-mile, but it takes you to a large alpine beauty.

The hike up to Hurricane Pass is a strenuous two miles beyond Sunset Lake. The trail is well built, and if you have the time and energy, it's worth every step. At the top of Hurricane Pass is one of the best views of the Grand Teton in the entire range. You can also look down on Schoolroom Glacier. Far below, you'll see the South Fork of Cascade Canyon. On our hike up Hurricane Pass we saw a half-dozen bighorn sheep near the top.

Final Thoughts

For hikers who can't get enough and are interested in an even longer trek, you can take this trail all the way to Jenny Lake. From the Basin Lake, head north to Sunset Lake, then on to Hurricane Pass. From here, the trail goes over the crest of the Tetons and down Cascade Canyon to Jenny Lake. You'll have to arrange a shuttle back, but it will be a trip you will remember for years to come. Expect to hike three days and at least two nights for a fairly leisurely pace. Overnight permits are not needed in the wilderness area. Pick up permits ahead of time if you plan to spend the night within the park boundaries.

When we made this hike, we met a father with his six sons hiking from the South Teton Creek Trailhead to Jenny Lake all in one day—more than twenty miles. The youngest boy was about eleven. Their biggest worries were "When do we eat lunch?" and "Are we on schedule? We don't want Mom waiting for us at Jenny Lake." When we met them, they were an hour ahead of schedule.

27 Cascade Canyon/ Lake Solitude

Main Attractions: Enchanting canyon with beautiful views of the mountains, easy walking up to the forks of the canyon, wildlife-viewing, berry-picking, beautiful alpine lake, and nice campsites for backpackers.

Getting There: From the Moose Visitor Center, drive 7 miles north on the Teton Park Road to South Jenny Lake Junction. Park near the Jenny Lake Visitor Center. To cut out 2 miles each way for young hikers, it's a good idea to take the shuttle boat across the lake. The hike up the canyon starts just up from Inspiration Point.

Trail Distance: From the boat dock on the west side of the lake it is .9-mile up to Inspiration Point. From the west boat dock to the forks of Cascade Canyon is 4.5 miles. From the west boat dock to Lake Solitude is 7.2 miles.

Elevation Gain/Loss: 1,057 feet up to the forks of the canyon; another 1,200 feet up to Lake Solitude

How Strenuous: Moderate hiking to the forks of the canyon; strenuous up to Lake Solitude. If your toddlers or preschoolers can make it up to Inspiration Point, then you can probably take them a little way up the canyon. Children ten years old and up should do okay beyond the forks.

When to Go: July to October for the main canyon; check at the visitor center for snow on the trail up to Lake Solitude

Animals to Watch For: Marmots and pikas in abundance, squirrels, moose, deer, songbirds, occasionally black bears

Cascade Canyon is regarded by many as the most beautiful hike in the Tetons. That's hard to dispute. The

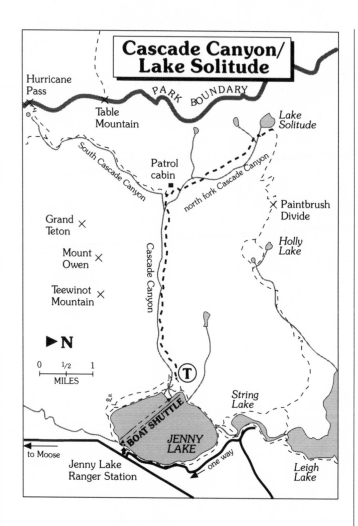

Cascade Canyon/ Lake Solitude

Hurricane Pass

PARK BOUNDARY

Table Mountain

Lake Solitude

South Cascade Canyon

Patrol cabin

north fork Cascade Canyon

Grand × Teton

Mount × Owen

Teewinot × Mountain

Cascade Canyon

× Paintbrush Divide

Holly Lake

▶N

| 0 | ½ | 1 |

MILES

T

String Lake

BOAT SHUTTLE

to Moose

Jenny Lake Ranger Station

JENNY LAKE

one way

Leigh Lake

trail certainly ranks up there with the Alaska Basin Trail and Death Canyon, also known for their beauty.

My family found the canyon enchanting. Whenever we passed through rocky sections on the trail we were greeted by the bleats of pikas and the curious stares of marmots. The canyon passes beside huge peaks, some towering a mile above. You are treated to views of Mount Owen, Teewinot, and Grand Teton. The view

Lake Solitude, at the top of the North Fork of Cascade Canyon, is surrounded by steep canyon walls.

looking south from Lake Solitude is "awesome," to quote my kids. It's definitely worth the effort up.

On the down side, be ready for black flies. On warm summer days the little beasties patrol the trail with a vengeance.

From the boat dock on the west side of the lake, it's about .9-mile and four hundred feet up a rocky trail to Inspiration Point. After Inspiration Point, the trail climbs a bit more to the mouth of the canyon. The next 3.5 miles to the forks is a gentle and gradual upward slope. In most cases the elevation increase is hardly noticeable.

Cascade Canyon is a super example of glacial carving. The canyon was dished out by glaciers that left the bottom with wide floors and steep walls. Avalanches and rockslides are continually working to reshape the canyon. As you walk along the trail, look for large trees snapped off several feet up at the snow line.

In mid- to late summer, look for wild raspberries among the rocks. Huckleberries hang out in the forested areas. The berries can be very plentiful some years. A big huckleberry patch can be a nice destination for families with smaller children not planning to go far. Families with older children may want to limit berry-picking in order to achieve more distant goals. Remember that animals depend on the berries for their diet—be sure to leave plenty behind for them!

Moose inhabit the willow-brush areas along the creek. Look for a large brown head moving above the fields of green brush.

About midway up the canyon are some nice waterfalls on the south side. These can be somewhat diminished by late summer. These falls tumble down from snowfields in the gaps between Teewinot Mountain, Mount Owen, and Grand Teton.

After you reach the forks, walk about one hundred yards up the south fork trail to catch a glimpse of a very large cascade. I don't recommend the trail beyond this for family hiking. This trail is best appreciated by experienced backpackers willing to invest two or three days.

The hike up the north fork climbs more than one thousand feet in the next three miles on its way to Lake Solitude. This is alpine country. Talus slopes dominate the canyon. Trees are scrubby and wildflowers are plentiful. Besides pikas and marmots, look for songbirds. About a mile up the north fork canyon are some nice campsites for backpackers. One group site has a food box to keep critters, particularly black bears, from making a mess of your camp chow.

Don't forget to turn around and look back down the canyon occasionally. The stunning view of the mountains, especially Grand Teton, will help renew your energy for the last little steep section up to the lake. The trail climbs a steep moraine just before you arrive at the lake. There are some nice views from the north side of the lake. Please stay on established trails in this area to keep from harming the fragile plant life.

Kid Comments

I've never seen so many pikas and marmots.

Beyond the lake, the trail climbs two miles and seventeen hundred feet to Paintbrush Divide. This route is strenuous and only for hikers in good shape. Expect large snowfields at the divide. Ice axes may be needed as late as July to go over the pass. There is no water beyond Lake Solitude for about four miles. I do not recommend this route for families with children younger than the teens.

Final Thoughts

The trail to Lake Solitude is usually snow-free by the first week in July. The ice is usually gone from the lake by the second week in July. Some years, though, snow can linger on the trail much later. Play it safe and ask ahead at the Jenny Lake Ranger Station before you try an early- or late-season hike. Wildflowers are usually best in late July to early August. In dry years these times are pushed up by a week or so.

Death Canyon

28

Main Attractions: Scenic views, cascading water, beautiful upper mountain canyon, wild raspberries, and wildlife-viewing

Getting There: The trailhead is off the Moose-Wilson Road 3 miles south of Moose. Drive 3 miles southwest on the Moose-Wilson Road from Moose and turn right (west) at the Death Canyon trailhead sign on a narrow paved road. After a half-mile the road becomes a bumpy dirt road for another half-mile. There are a few overflow parking areas before you get to the trailhead.

Trail Distance: .9-mile up to the Phelps Lake overlook; 3.5 miles up to where the canyon levels off; 4 miles to a patrol cabin

Elevation Gain/Loss: 400 feet up to the Phelps Lake overlook, then 400 feet down to the mouth of Death Canyon; 1,000 feet up to the level area of Death Canyon

How Strenuous: Moderately tough hiking up to the Phelps Lake overlook; strenuous up Death Canyon. Toddlers and preschoolers accustomed to walking should enjoy the trip up to the Phelps Lake overlook. Hiking beyond the overlook is not recommended for toddlers and preschoolers.

When to Go: After the snows are gone in late May or mid-June to October

Animals to Watch For: Lots of marmots, squirrels, moose, deer, songbirds, and pikas

This hike offers families a few different options depending on ability and energy level. The short hike up to the Phelps Lake overlook climaxes with a terrific view of the park's fourth largest lake. If you plan to go the entire 3.5 miles but your children poop out partway up

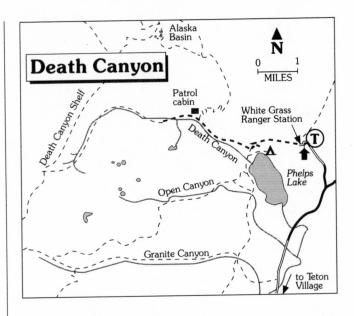

the canyon, you can still make them feel good by telling them they saw the giant cascading stream. And if you make it to where the canyon levels and becomes easy hiking again, you'll be treated to an Edenlike beauty with giant trees and transparent water.

The hike up to the Phelps Lake overlook takes you through stands of lodgepole pine and across footbridges that span several small streams. This is a wet area, especially in the early spring. Because of all the water, you'll find thick vegetation here not found in other parts of the park.

The trail soon leaves the woods and enters a meadow area. This area is fringed with aspens and scrubs. It is also touched with the color of a variety of wildflowers. Occasionally you will pass by some massive Douglas fir trees. We were impressed by one more than three feet wide that forked about thirty feet up. On our hike up we met a three-foot-long snake crossing the trail.

The trail is mostly a gradual incline until just before the overlook, when it climbs more steeply. When you

All-Day and Overnight Hikes

come to the overlook, stop awhile, sit on one of the large rocks, and take in the view. Phelps Lake is about 1.5 miles long and more than 150 feet deep. On the far side of the lake you can see several buildings. This is the JY Ranch. The ranch was originally established by Louis H. Joy in 1908 as one of the first dude ranches in Jackson Hole. It is now owned by the Rockefeller family.

The lake was named by F. V. Hayden after a trapper named Phelps. His full name is unknown. Historians believe Phillips Canyon and Phillips Pass are also named for the same trapper, whose name was misspelled in the diary of Hayden's scout, Beaver Dick Leigh.

From the overlook, the trail switchbacks down about four hundred feet to near the lake. Near the lake the trail forks. The trail heading south, the Valley Trail, goes around the west side of the lake. The trail to the right heads up Death Canyon and along its creek. As you approach the creek, look off to your right and up the cliff walls for a small but very high waterfall. This fall becomes a mere trickle in late summer.

The first quarter-mile is fairly easy hiking and brings you near the creek and into some huge fir and spruce trees. Watch for yellow-bellied marmots perched on the large boulders. If they see you as you approach, they often duck into their holes. We found that if we stood and waited a minute, their curiosity would get the better of them and they would soon pop back out to have a look. Some were so curious that they would walk within a few feet of us. It seems that we were spied on by marmots at every rest stop with large boulders nearby. The higher up the canyon we were, the more marmots there seemed to be. At our lunch break where the canyon levels off, we must have counted a half dozen marmots sneaking over to check us out.

The trail up the canyon climbs steadily for about a half-mile and then begins to switchback. About where the switchbacks begin, the creek begins to roar. This is a sight to see. At this height, huge boulders clog the

Kid Comments

The name of that marmot is Lazy, because it just lays there and the other one is Heidi, because it likes to hide.

A Death Canyon hiker comes upon a moose. Both moose and hiker were warily making their way up the steep trail to the flat canyon above.

canyon. White water roars over and around the steep drop. This wonderful scene continues for about a quarter of a mile.

At the top of the switchbacks the canyon narrows into a tight V or portal before opening up into a wide U-shaped canyon. This level section of the canyon is a popular overnight destination for backpackers. There are several very nice campsites available in this section of the canyon beyond a small patrol cabin.

The patrol cabin is used by trail maintenance crews when they work in Death Canyon. Past the cabin the trail forks. The trail to the right connects with the Alaska Basin Trail and passes by Static Peak. Beyond this fork the canyon opens up into a large meadow of willows and brush where the creek meanders slowly through. Look for moose grazing in this meadow area. The size of this canyon's basin is very impressive. Farther up the basin, look for waterfalls, especially on the south side, cascading down into the canyon.

Raspberries grow in abundance along the trail, especially high in the canyon. The berries ripen in late summer. But when summer actually comes to the Tetons varies from year to year—anytime from early June to mid-July.

This trail is often traveled by moose heading up to the lush upper canyon or down to Phelps Lake. Moose usually retreat off the trail at the sight of people. But, as in our case, one can meet with a cow and calf along the switchbacks. Momma plus baby moose is a dangerous combination to be around. You can be very patient and wait until the animal hikes to the top and disappears into the lush willows of the upper canyon, or you can call it a hike and head back down. If the moose is coming down the canyon, the poor animal is probably in for a frustrating day, because it will meet several hikers going up. If possible, find a place to safely scramble out of its way to a safe distance of twenty or more yards and let it pass you by.

Final Thoughts

This is a popular trail. To avoid most of the crowds, go during the week and start early in the morning. Also, take plenty of water for the tough hike up the canyon. Hot summer days can make this trail much tougher. Many people who start late in the day end up soaking in the cool stream halfway up the canyon. Also remember to reserve some energy for the hike back up to the Phelps Lake overlook.

Granite Canyon Trail

29

Main Attractions: Beautiful, scenic canyon with several very nice backcountry campsites; wildflowers abound in the upper canyon; waterfalls and wildlife-viewing

Getting There: Drive 2 miles north of Teton Village on the Moose-Wilson Road. The Granite Canyon Trail parking area is on the left. The trail parking area is 6 miles southwest of Moose.

Trail Distance: 1.6 miles to the junction with the Valley Trail; about 2.5 miles to the start of the camping area; 6.3 miles to patrol cabin and junction with Rendezvous Mountain Trail; 8.8 miles to Marion Lake

Elevation Gain/Loss: Climbs 1,500 feet from trailhead to patrol cabin

How Strenuous: Between moderate and strenuous, depending on how far up you go. Not recommended for toddlers. Preschoolers may enjoy going up a couple of miles to the first good berry patch.

When to Go: June for the lower elevations; July to October for hiking to the upper canyon

Animals to Watch For: Songbirds, moose, deer, and small mammals

Granite Canyon has a little bit of everything that makes the canyons of the Tetons interesting to hike. The first four or five miles are heavily forested with very high, steep walls of rock, especially on the south side. Granite Creek—a good-sized stream—rushes down the canyon to be used for irrigation and eventually meets up with Fish Creek. The creek cascades out of the canyon mouth near the trailside.

The canyon's forest is occasionally broken by

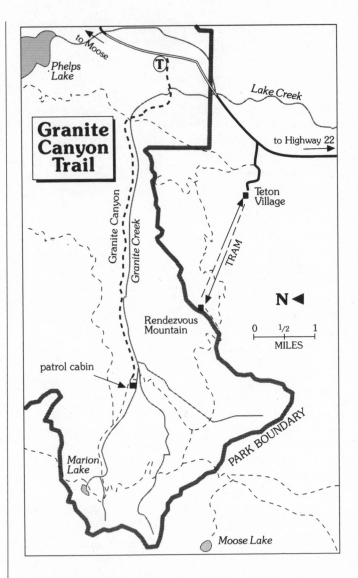

Granite
Canyon
Trail

Phelps
Lake

to Moose

Lake Creek

to Highway 22

Granite Canyon

Granite Creek

Teton
Village

TRAM

N ◀

Rendezvous
Mountain

0   ½   1
MILES

patrol cabin

Marion
Lake

PARK BOUNDARY

Moose Lake

sections of brushy talus-covered rockslides. Look for pikas and marmots in these rocky areas.

Large patches of huckleberries often slowed down our progress in the canyon. Once you get started eating the berries, it's hard not to stop at each berry patch along the trail. Wild raspberries can also be found in the rocky areas. Enjoy them, but be sure to leave plenty of berries behind for the animals who eat them to help fatten up for winter.

The trail starts out easy enough then climbs over some small moraines to enter the canyon. From here on up the trail has a mostly gentle upward climb until it reaches the patrol cabin near the junction with the Rendezvous Mountain Trail.

About a half-mile from the mouth of the canyon the camping zone begins. This is a popular trail for backpackers who don't want to hike very far to reach a camping area. For this reason, it's a nice destination for family backpackers. There are several established campsites along the way, and hikers are likely to spot a few tents off the trail.

Families day hiking with small children may want to turn around a few miles up. Pick a nice overlook of Granite Creek or an impressive view of the surrounding canyon walls as a nice turnaround point, so that your children don't feel that your're just turning around because they pooped out.

If your group has the energy to go farther, there are two very nice attractions up ahead. One that children find interesting is the rustic patrol cabin near the Middle and North forks of the creek. These backcountry patrol cabins are used by the Park Service work crews when they are doing trail maintenance. They are also used by rangers doing overnight checkups on areas. My children usually wonder out loud what it would be like to live year-round in such a place.

Just past the patrol cabin, on the route to Rendezvous Mountain, a bridge crosses the stream. Look upstream from the bridge to see a pretty little waterfall.

For the next couple of miles up the Rendezvous Mountain trail, the wildflowers are sensational. Large stretches of meadow are filled with one of the park's best displays.

The other trail up the North Fork of the canyon

Kid Comments
•••••••••••••

This trail sure has a lot of huckleberries. I don't want to stop eating them.

*Children often find backcountry patrol cabins, such as this one along the
Granite Canyon Trail, an interesting sight.*

takes you to beautiful Marion Lake. This is 8.8 miles from the trailhead, so I usually recommend that families take the Aerial Tram from Teton Village if the lake is their destination. The tram route, although more strenuous, trims off about four miles from the round trip.

Final Thoughts

Look for interesting natural forces at work in the canyon. The obvious ones are snow avalanches that have snapped off large trees about five or six feet up, where the snow level was. Also look for areas where rock- and mudslides have come down to change the canyon's bottom.

30 Green Lakes

Main Attractions: Beautiful subalpine lakes tucked in against the tops of the mountains, wildlife-viewing, scenic views, abundant wildflowers, and good trout fishing

Getting There: Drive 5.5 miles north of Driggs, Idaho, on Highway 33. When the highway makes a ninety-degree turn west, continue going straight. Take the very next road right (east)—there are signs to North and South Leigh Creek trails. The road soon becomes gravel. Drive 2.5 miles and turn left (north) at the sign for North Leigh Creek. Drive about 5 miles to the end of the road and a parking area at the trailhead.

Trail Distance: 12.5 miles round-trip to the first lake. If you explore farther up the canyon to the other lakes, add another 2 miles.

Elevation Gain/Loss: Gains about 2,000 feet in the first 4 miles, then drops about 400 feet down to the first lake. On the way back you gain 400 feet and drop 2,000 feet.

How Strenuous: Strenuous going up. About 3 to 3.5 hours up and 2 to 2.5 hours back. Not recommended for toddlers and preschoolers.

When to Go: Usually after the first of July to October. Snow can linger on the ridge next to Green Mountain into midsummer.

Animals to Watch For: Deer, elk, moose, songbirds, ospreys on the lake, and small mammals

This is beautiful wilderness hiking in the upper west side—the Idaho side—of the Teton Range. The trail seems to have it all. The Green Lakes hike is a good all-day hike or overnight backpacking trip. It's not a beginner trail, but I have seen seven- and eight-year-olds make the trip just fine.

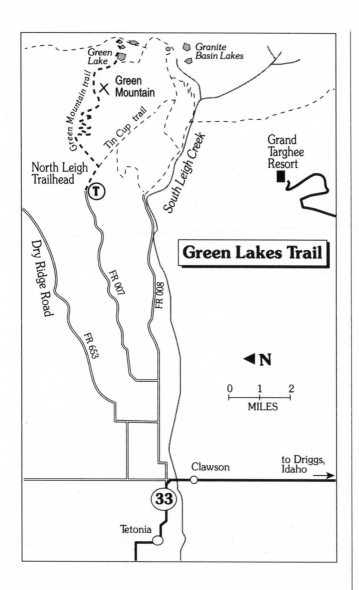

The trail crosses a footbridge over Tin Cup Creek and almost immediately enters the Jedediah Smith Wilderness Area. The wilderness is named after the famous fur trapper, Jedediah Strong Smith, who roamed throughout the West in the 1820s and early

Hikers pause for lunch at Green Lake, on the western side of the Tetons.

1830s. He was a partner to David Jackson, the man for whom Jackson Hole is named. Smith was reputed to be the first man to travel overland to California. In 1831 he was killed by Comanches on the Santa Fe Trail.

The trail quickly begins its uphill climb to the Green Mountain ridge. Most of the trail is very well made. The grades are not too steep, and switchbacks help manage the climb up the side of the mountain.

For the first mile the trail takes you through thick lodgepole and fir forest. There are also some huckleberries to watch for in mid- to late summer. These small bluish purple berries look a lot like miniature blueberries. If you find any, try to save the picking for the return hike, or you may take all day to get up the mountain.

As the trail climbs higher, it takes you through some patches of aspens. Soon the trail begins some wide switchbacks through open treeless areas. The wildflowers here are superb, especially in mid- to late July.

After about four miles of steady climbing and switchbacking, the trail reaches a ridge and levels off for about .25-mile. This is as high as you'll get. Pause and look out over the Teton Valley to the west. To the east and south are nice views of neighboring mountains. Some years the snow lingers on this ridge until mid-July. This can make the trip down the other side too dangerous for inexperienced snow hikers.

The trail drops down the northeast side of the ridge in a series of switchbacks that go on for about .5-mile. Within another half-mile you arrive at the first Green Lake.

What a gorgeous sight. While we sat and ate lunch we saw scores of trout leaping from the water. On the far side of the lake we watched an osprey, some call them "fish hawks," diving into the water for its lunch. If you come to spend the night, there is a nice campsite on the northeast side of the lake.

There are three more lakes above the first. All three are within about 1.5 miles from the first. These lakes

Kid Comments
• • • • • • • • • • • • • •
This hike was worth it—this lake is just beautiful!

are about half the size of the first lake. They are just as beautiful but, as near as we could tell, don't have fish.

The return trip is fairly easy once you get past the steep switchbacks on the northeast side of the ridge.

Final Thoughts

Although you begin this trail on the Idaho side, the entire hike is well within Wyoming, and anglers will need a Wyoming state license.

A nice breeze will keep biting flies and mosquitoes at bay, but when the wind calms, have your repellent ready.

Hermitage Point Trail

Main Attractions: Wildlife-viewing, superb scenic views of Jackson Lake and the Teton Range beyond, backcountry camping, and mostly easy walking

Getting There: From the Jackson Lake Junction, drive north 5.5 miles to the junction with Colter Bay and turn left (west). Drive past the visitor center and park in the parking lot near the marina. The trailhead is at the south end of the marina parking lot.

Trail Distance: 9.5 to 10 miles round-trip, depending on the routes you take

Elevation Gain/Loss: 100 feet up and down

How Strenuous: The trail is easy, but the distance makes this a moderate hike. If you have toddlers and preschoolers, it's best to just stick to the Swan Lake and Heron Pond areas

When to Go: Early May to late October. This area is a good fall destination because it is off-limits to hunting.

Animals to Watch For: Swans, geese, pelicans, herons, and other waterfowl; songbirds, eagles, ospreys; moose, deer, elk, red squirrels, and other small mammals

Maps and Information: A helpful map of these trails is available at the Colter Bay Visitor Center

It is difficult to hike this entire trail and not see several squirrels, swans, pelicans, and deer. If you go in the early morning or in the evening, you are almost certain to see some of the bigger animals.

This is also a great trail for novice backpackers. The mostly flat, easy hiking will be appreciated by children who are used to day hiking where you carry little more

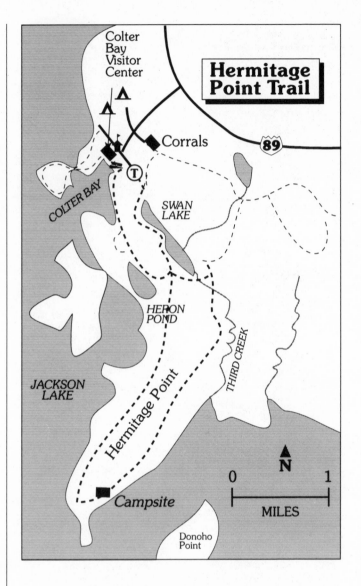

than a few snacks and a water bottle. You can obtain a free backcountry permit at the Colter Bay Visitor Center. There is a backcountry campsite on the southeast side of the point. This site is little more than a metal storage box to keep food away from critters.

The trail begins from the marina parking lot and immediately offers two routes. This is only the beginning of the maze of trails throughout the area. The trail on your right follows along Colter Bay. I suggest taking this route, because the other is frequently used by horseback riders.

For the first .4-mile, the trail follows along the water and has some great views of Mount Moran to the west. The trail forks at the .5-mile mark. The left route goes to Swan Lake, and the right heads to Heron Pond. Stay right to go around Hermitage Point in a counterclockwise route.

The trail leaves Colter Bay and enters a thick lodgepole pine forest. Red squirrels often "cuss" at you as you enter their territory. In the fall, the squirrels are so intent on gathering their store of pinecones for the coming winter that they will pass right in front of you, pretending you aren't there.

After a mile you come to Heron Pond. Just beyond the patches of water lilies you should spot a variety of waterfowl. We also saw here a very large bald eagle flying overhead. Beyond the pond, 1.4 miles from the trailhead, is another trail junction. The trail to your left heads over to the upper end of Swan Lake. Stick right to go to Hermitage Point.

The trail continues through thick lodgepole pine forest for the next three miles. Occasionally you'll get a glimpse of Jackson Lake to the northwest. About three miles past Heron Pond the trail draws near the lake and offers stunning views of the Tetons with the lake in the foreground. When you come to some large sagebrush areas, you are near the point. A spur trail heads off to a hitching post near the water. We found it to be a good place to let the kids splash around in the water. Because the water is shallow for a good distance in this spot, it is surprisingly warm in the summer.

The trail forks again, with one loop going to the very tip of Hermitage Point, while the cutoff continues around to the southeast side. About .25-mile from the point is the backcountry campsite. This campsite is also

Kid Comments
....
This is a long trail, I'm glad it's flat.

Children wade in the water of Jackson Lake along the Hermitage Point Trail.

used by boaters. As with most campsites, it is used less on weekdays.

On the southeast side of the point you can see across the lake to the Jackson Lake Dam. The large island to the southeast is Donoho Point. Donoho Point gets its name from a trapper who lived there at the turn of the century. The point became an island after the Jackson Lake Dam was built and raised the water level. Hermitage Point is named after a now-unknown man who gathered a great number of logs on the point to build a lodge or hermitage. After the dam was built, however, the builder floated the logs down the river and sold them. Colter Bay was also created by the rise in the lake's water level. The bay is named after John Colter, perhaps the first white man to visit Jackson Hole. Colter was a fur trapper who traveled through the valley during the winter of 1807–1808.

A mile from the point the trail heads away from the

water. When you near Third Creek you are presented with some more trail connections. Be sure not to miss the trail along Swan Lake. The lake usually has waterfowl—deer, elk, and moose visit off and on during the day and particularly during the morning and evening.

Beyond Swan Lake, it's about .6-mile back to the parking lot.

Final Thoughts

Because of the marshy nature of the area, mosquitoes and black flies can be rough through the summer. Put repellent on before you hike to eliminate the bug factor. This can also be a hotter hike if you're used to the mountain trails, so bring along plenty of water.

32 | Marion Lake via Tram

Main Attractions: Great scenic views, a fun tram ride, wildlife-viewing, wildflowers, backcountry camping, and a beautiful alpine lake

Getting There: Drive west on Highway 22 from Jackson, turn right on the Teton Village Road, and follow the signs to the Jackson Hole ski area. Park in the lot near the tram. After you take the tram to the top of Rendezvous Mountain, walk south down the mountain road. The trailhead sign to Marion Lake and Granite Canyon is on the right about .25-mile from the tram.

Trail Distance: Round-trip is 12.5 miles

Elevation Gain/Loss: The trail starts out at 10,450 feet and drops to about 8,800 feet before climbing up and down about 400 feet over two ridges. Marion Lake sits at 9,240 feet.

How Strenuous: Mostly moderate with some strenuous sections. Not recommended for toddlers and preschoolers. It's best if your family is in good physical condition.

When to Go: Usually after the first of July through October. Wildflowers are usually best in late July to early August.

Animals to Watch For: Look for moose, deer, bear, foxes, songbirds, and small mammals

This is a trail that nearly has it all. Many hikers use this trail as an easy way to begin hiking the Teton Crest Trail. For families, this can be a rewarding all-day hike or a memorable backpacking trip.

If you intend to hike to the lake and back in one day, be sure to leave early in order to catch the tram ride down. The tram quits running by 7:30 P.M. on most summer days. The round trip takes most families around eight hours to complete.

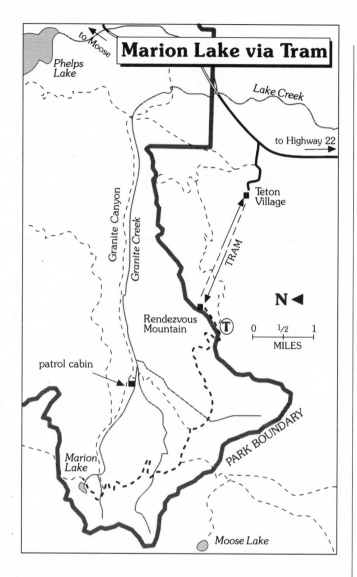

There are several very nice backcountry campsites on the way up to the lake, and two campsites next to Marion Lake. Backcountry camping permits from the park are required. If you want to avoid hauling a hefty pack up the switchbacks to the lake, you can camp down in the canyon and stash your pack while you hike up to the lake.

Kicking off the shoes and soaking in the sight of Marion Lake.

The first four miles of the hike are almost easy. The walking is mostly downhill and the trail is well made. Around the third mile you will come into large open meadows. During midsummer, the wildflower displays here are fantastic. After about 3.5 miles you will come to a junction. The trail to your right goes down Granite Canyon. You will want to go left, on the Middle Fork Cutoff Trail. This trail connects up with the Teton Crest Trail after about .5-mile. The last two miles to Marion Lake include two uphill climbs separated by a downhill stretch. This section, although not too strenuous, can take the spring out of younger children.

Marion Lake is a beautiful jewel nestled against a 10,116-foot peak to the northwest. The lake is named after Marion Danford. Danford came to Jackson Hole in 1915 from Philadelphia. She eventually became the owner of the D Triangle Ranch.

The hike back to the tram looks harder than it really is. The well-engineered trail makes the fifteen-hundred-foot climb seem like much less. But, to be honest, the last .25-mile up the road to the tram does seem to take forever.

Remember to drink plenty of water, and take lots of snacks and pick-me-up candy for the youngsters.

Final Thoughts

Be sure to look up and down each of the creeks you cross along the trail. This is prime moose country. We spotted a group of four bull moose along the North Fork of Granite Creek on one hike to Marion Lake. Also keep an eye out for marmots and pikas in the rocky areas.

Remember to take along a sweater for each hiker on cool days. Temperatures at the top of Rendezvous Mountain can be twenty to thirty degrees cooler than those of the valley floor.

Kid Comments

I really liked seeing that bunch of moose so close to the trail, and the lake is very pretty.

33 Moose Creek

Main Attractions: Fishing, beaver dams, mountain meadows, waterfalls, and wildlife-viewing

Getting There: From Victor, Idaho, drive 3 miles southeast on Highway 33 and turn left on the Moose Creek Road; drive .3-mile and turn right (east) and drive to the end of the road and park

Trail Distance: 4.4 miles up to Moose Meadows; 5.8 miles to falls

Elevation Gain/Loss: Gains 800 feet from trailhead to Moose Meadows; trail climbs another 200 feet to the falls

How Strenuous: Moderately tough. Not recommended for toddlers and preschoolers.

When to Go: Late May to mid-June (when the snow is gone) through October. Avoid this trail during the hunting season.

Animals to Watch For: Moose, deer, waterfowl, eagles, beavers, and small mammals

The Moose Creek Trail offers a fun hike up a classic mountain canyon featuring a good-sized trout stream, beaver ponds, a large meadow, and a waterfall.

Moose Creek is on the west side of the Tetons in the Jedediah Smith Wilderness Area. The Jedediah Smith Wilderness borders Grand Teton National Park on the west and contains some of the area's best backcountry.

The trail starts out tough for the first eighth of a mile until it climbs up to an old dirt road along the south side of the creek. From here the next mile or so is fairly easy hiking. The road eventually narrows down to a trail. The canyon is thickly forested with Douglas fir, spruce, and lodgepole pine. Willow brush clogs the creek bottoms.

The trail crosses the creek on a nice footbridge at the

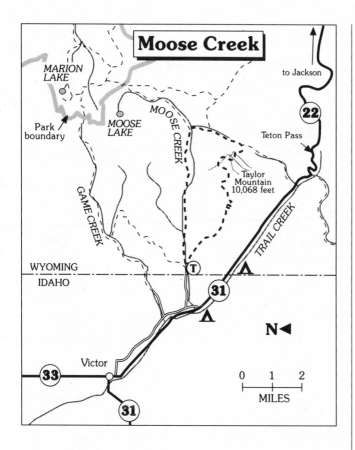

Moose Creek

MARION LAKE

Park boundary

MOOSE LAKE

MOOSE CREEK

GAME CREEK

to Jackson

Teton Pass

Taylor Mountain 10,068 feet

TRAIL CREEK

WYOMING

IDAHO

Victor

N◄

0   1   2
MILES

second mile. If at first you don't spot the bridge, keep looking. (The horseback riders usually walk through the water.) After the bridge, the trail climbs sharply for a quarter of a mile. At the three-mile mark is a small meadow fed by a spring and backed up by some busy beavers. If your collective legs are already tired, this is a good turnaround point. There are some eight- to twelve-inch brook trout hiding in the shadows of this spring water. Be forewarned, though—catching these beauties is not a piece of cake. Because the water is crystal clear and only a foot or so deep, the trout are easily spooked. Try the riffles below the beaver dams or pools with overhanging brush.

Moose Creek Falls thunders down a narrow crack in the canyon walls.

Another 1.4 miles up the canyon the trail comes to Moose Meadows. This huge meadow is several acres wide. The area is laced with beaver channels and slack water. As you approach the meadows, keep a look out for waterfowl. We spotted a blue heron and several ducks. Moose, deer, and elk also frequent the area. If you go down to the meadow, you should be able to spot a classic beaver lodge.

Fishing in this meadow can be just as challenging as at the lower meadows. You will often see the trout after you've spooked them. Try to stand back a distance from the pools and riffles where the fish should be lying, so as not to spook them.

This can be a nice place for backpackers to spend the night. There are a few good campsites, especially on the far side of the meadow.

For hikers with extra energy, there's a nice waterfall 1.4 miles up the trail. Just past the meadow the trail crosses the creek. There is no bridge here, so if you want to go farther, plan to slosh through the water. I suggest bringing along Aquasocks or lightweight sandals to put on for the crossing. Beyond the wet crossing the trail begins to climb and continues a steady climb. The creek begins to make a lot more noise as it cascades down the canyon. When the trail takes you through a rocky section, watch the creek canyon from the trail for a narrow gap that the water falls through.

Grand Teton National Park is about 1.7 miles from the falls. The trail forks about .5-mile before the park boundary. The trail following the creek hooks west and leads up to beautiful Moose Lake. Special regulations are in force to protect the delicate subalpine area around Moose Lake. No camping with stock animals or stock grazing, and no campfires are allowed. If you wish to camp here, bring along a pack stove.

Final Thoughts

This trail is heavily used by horseback riders. There is a horse outfitter and ranch at the mouth of the canyon. If you plan to hike this trail, expect to meet

Kid Comments

The dog is scaring away all the fish.

horses. Remember to step well off the trail to let horses by. If you are on a slope, step to the downhill side so that if a stumble should occur, it won't be under a passing horse.

Because this is national forest land, there is a possibility of meeting domestic sheep grazing in some areas.

South Leigh Creek/ Granite Basin Lakes

Main Attractions: Beautiful canyon stream, fishing, wildlife-viewing, and if you've got the energy to climb up the canyon you will see some stunning alpine lakes and mountain vistas

Getting There: From Driggs, Idaho, drive 5.5 miles north on Highway 33. As the highway takes a ninety-degree turn to the left (west), turn off the highway, continuing north. Turn right (east) at the next road. There should be signs for North and South Leigh trails. The road soon becomes gravel. Continue on this road for 7 miles to the trailhead.

Trail Distance: 1.4 miles to the Andy Stone Trail junction; 2.7 miles to the next trail junction; 4 miles to the switchbacks; and 7.7 miles to Granite Basin

Elevation Gain/Loss: 150-foot rise from trailhead to switchbacks; more than 2,500 feet up from creek bottom to Granite Basin. The trailhead is at 7,000 feet.

How Strenuous: Mostly easy for the first 4 miles from the trailhead to switchbacks; very strenuous up the switchbacks to Granite Basin. Not recommended for toddlers and preschoolers.

When to Go: June to October if you only want to hike the creek bottom; late June or early July to October for Granite Basin

Animals to Watch For: Small mammals, moose, songbirds, elk, deer, bear, waterfowl in the basin lakes

This is a trail with a split personality. The first four miles that parallel South Leigh Creek are gentle and fairly easy walking. But if you are interested in taking off out of the canyon, beware! These trails climb nearly to the top of the range.

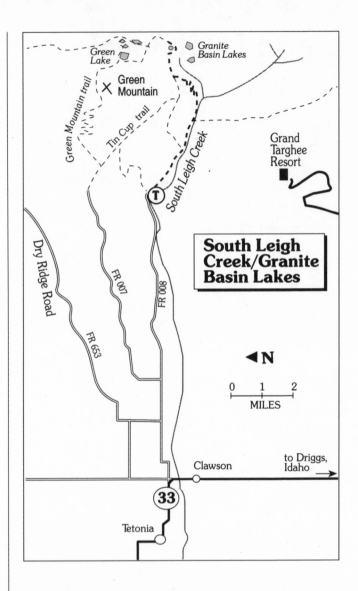

Green Lake

Granite Basin Lakes

Green Mountain trail

× Green Mountain

Tin Cup trail

South Leigh Creek

Grand Targhee Resort

South Leigh Creek/Granite Basin Lakes

Dry Ridge Road

FR 007

FR 008

FR 653

◀ N

0   1   2
MILES

to Driggs, Idaho →

Clawson

(33)

Tetonia

Because of the tough climb, I only recommend the creekside trail for most families. The trail is obviously less used up the canyon.

This canyon has more streams than are shown on the map. The trail crosses three good-sized streams in the first 1.3 miles before you reach the Andy Stone Trail junction. Most of these streams are still flowing in mid-summer; by late August, some of them will only be muddy spots. Because of all the water, much of the summer here is a fight with biting insects. Come prepared for black flies and mosquitoes.

The canyon is heavily forested with fir and spruce. The trail passes through occasional meadows that are a mass of wildflowers.

The trail only draws near to the main creek a few times. If you wish to wade or fish the stream, there are a couple of nice places about three miles down the trail and near the junction with the trail to Teton Creek. At this junction there is a large stock/foot bridge over the creek. The water is very cold during the first part of the summer. Fishing is marginal. I suggest trying flies or salmon eggs.

If you wish to spend the night, there is a large campsite at the bottom of the switchbacks. There are also some other nice spots at the meadows before the footbridge. The nice thing about backpacking is that you don't need much flat ground to make a decent camp.

At the top of this canyon await beautiful alpine basin lakes and views to rival any in the Tetons. On the hike up you will see the Grand Teton towering over the ridge. These lakes once boasted great trout fishing, but winterkill and overfishing have taken their toll—don't bother hauling up your gear. The three largest lakes are from three to five acres in size. Beautiful snowmelt creeks cascade down the surrounding cliffs to fill the lakes each spring.

If you have desires to see the Granite Basin lakes, there are two routes. Both are strenuous, and it depends on how you like your poison: all at once or spread out a distance. The Andy Stone Trail climbs right up the side of the canyon with only a few level stretches to let you catch your breath. The other route, a switchback trail at the end of the canyon, seems to take forever to get you to the top. But the switchbacks are well engineered so as not to bite off huge elevation gains at each turn.

Kid Comments

This is a nice big campground.

One of the alpine lakes that dot the top of Granite Basin, high above South Leigh Creek on the west side of the Tetons.

Nevertheless, you can't sugarcoat a twenty-five-hundred-foot elevation gain in 3.7 miles of trail. This part of the trail is only for experienced hiking families who are in good condition. Otherwise, you will find yourself exhausted and disappointed at never reaching the top.

If you are serious about getting to the top, you may want to spend the night at the base of the switchbacks and rise early and hike to the top in the cool of the day. Take plenty of drinking water and snacks. Don't expect to go much faster than 1.5 miles per hour.

Final Thoughts

Summer comes later in high Granite Basin. Most years the trail is still snowcovered until July 4 or later.

Watch out for stinging nettle along the banks of the creek.

Surprise Lake/ Amphitheater Lake

Main Attractions: Fantastic scenic views of Jackson Hole and two subalpine lakes tucked in against the surrounding peaks, wildlife-viewing, wildflowers, and cascading streams

Getting There: Drive 7.5 miles north of the Moose Visitor Center on the Teton Park Road and turn left (west) at the sign for Lupine Meadows. This unpaved road is a mile south of the South Jenny Lake Junction. Follow the road about 1.5 miles to a parking area. There is a restroom at the trailhead.

Trail Distance: 9.6 miles round-trip. It is 4.9 miles to Surprise Lake and .2-mile farther to Amphitheater Lake. Garnet Canyon is a spur trail; its junction is 3 miles up. The mouth of the canyon is 1.1 miles from the junction.

Elevation Gain/Loss: 2,958 feet up from the parking lot

How Strenuous: Strenuous. Not recommended for toddlers or preschoolers. Beyond the third mile may be too difficult for children under age 8 or 9.

When to Go: The snow is usually gone from the trail after mid-July, but check at the visitor center just in case

Animals to Watch For: Deer, elk, moose (in the lower meadow area), small mammals, eagles, songbirds in the upper reaches

Any hike that gains just under a thousand feet a mile is going to cause you to huff and puff and sweat. This is not a beginner's trail. But any family in average shape without small children should do fine. Small children may enjoy the first 2.5 to 3 miles, where the trail climbs to a marvelous view of Taggart and Bradley lakes far

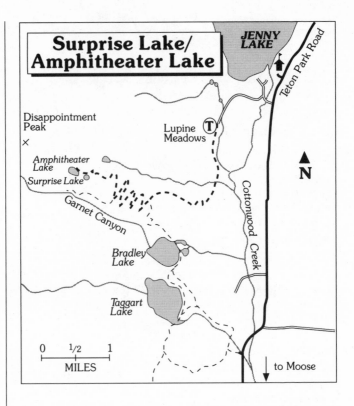

Surprise Lake/ Amphitheater Lake

JENNY LAKE

Teton Park Road

Disappointment Peak
×

Lupine Meadows (T)

Amphitheater Lake
Surprise Lake

N

Garnet Canyon

Cottonwood Creek

Bradley Lake

Taggart Lake

0   1/2   1
MILES

to Moose

below and the valley beyond. Hikers will also be treated to an array of wildflowers along the treeless sections of the trail.

Don't let the workout scare you off, though, because this is one of the best hikes in the park. The trail is well made and doesn't try to gain the elevation too quickly. On weekends the trailhead parking lot often has dozens of cars. Many of the people slogging up the trail are carrying climbing gear—ropes and ice axes—in hopes of making it to the top of Grand Teton. Many of the climbers head up Garnet Canyon, which offers a nice sloping saddle from which to approach the peak. There are also backcountry campsites between Surprise and Amphitheater lakes.

The trail starts out almost flat for the first .3-mile as it heads south across Lupine Meadows. This area gets its name from the lavender-blue flower that blooms here in abundance. You will notice that this part of the trail was once paved and used as a nature trail by the park. Deer, elk, moose, and occasionally bison haunt the meadows and are most often seen in the morning and evenings.

The trail begins to make gentle climbs, and after about a half-mile crosses the creek fed by Teton Glacier some four thousand feet above. You notice that the color of the water is a milky blue-green. This color is the result of finely ground rock sediment from the glacier that remains suspended in the water.

The trail begins to climb for the next mile until it reaches a junction. The trail heading south, the Valley Trail, takes you to Bradley Lake. Continuing upward starts you on a long series of about eighteen switchbacks up the mountainside. There are clumps of trees every few hundred yards for resting out of the glare of the sun. Don't forget to bring along plenty of water. Take your time and enjoy the view. About 1 to 1.5 miles from the junction is a great place to take in the view of both Bradley and Taggart lakes far below, and Jackson Hole beyond. One switchback gives you a glimpse of most of Jenny Lake.

Near the three-mile mark, the trail joins the Garnet Canyon Trail. This trail takes you to a narrow V-shaped canyon with a large cascading stream. The first .3-mile is mostly flat. Beyond that point the trail climbs up the canyon. After 1.1 miles the hiking is considered "off-trail" hiking. To hike here, obtain more information at the Jenny Lake Ranger Station. This is a beautiful canyon with large cascades and falls. But families should conserve their energy and save this side trip for another day if they hope to make it to Amphitheater Lake.

From the Garnet Canyon Trail junction, it's a bit less than two miles to Surprise Lake. About .25-mile before you reach the lake, the trail levels off. From here you will get some nice views of the surrounding peaks. Surprise Lake sits at 9,300 feet, and it's a beauty. Take some time to get to know the lake. There's a footpath

Kid Comments
• • • • • • • • • • • •
Hey, there's snow up here! (Young girl on July 4.)

A hiker pauses to take in the view at Surprise Lake.

around the water if you want a look from the other side. From Surprise Lake it's only .2-mile to Amphitheater Lake. A small outlet stream cascades down from Amphitheater Lake into Surprise Lake. Amphitheater Lake at 9,698 feet has the added beauty of Disappointment Peak jutting up almost from the water's edge. After you see the lake, its name becomes obvious. Disappointment Peak, at 11,618 feet, was named by Phil Smith and Walter Harvey in 1925. They climbed the peak, thinking it would offer a good route to the Grand Teton, only to find a huge gulf between the two.

If you left early enough in the morning, eating lunch at Amphitheater Lake can be a very rewarding experience.

Beyond Amphitheater Lake, an "off-trail" trail heads over to the Teton Glacier. Hiking here is not advised for youngsters. If you want to go into this area, inquire at the Jenny Lake Ranger Station. The staff there can advise you of current conditions on this area.

The hike back down should take about half the time as the hike up. Take time to pause at some viewpoints and look out over the valley.

Final Thoughts

Caution your children about going too fast downhill. Downhill hiking often causes more injuries, blisters, and sore muscles. Because going downhill doesn't give you a cardiovascular workout, as going uphill does, we often skip more rest stops. But make sure to take at least a few rests to give those other muscles a break.

36 | Table Mountain

Main Attractions: Fantastic views of the western side of the Tetons, especially Grand Teton peak—seems as if you can reach out and touch it—and wildlife-viewing. This is a rewarding, nontechnical hike to the top of an 11,106-foot square-topped peak.

Getting There: From Victor, Idaho, drive 8 miles north on Highway 33 to Driggs. Turn right (east) at the main intersection, following the signs to Grand Targhee Ski Resort, drive 6 miles, and turn right onto a dirt road with a sign for Teton Campground. Drive 5 miles to the trailhead/parking lot for North Teton Trail.

Trail Distance: 12.5 miles to the top of the mountain and back

Elevation Gain/Loss: 4,100 feet, going up and down

How Strenuous: Strenuous. It is recommended that all hikers be in good condition. Not recommended for children under age ten (even though many younger than that often make it).

When to Go: Early July most years, to September or early October

Animals to Watch For: Moose, bighorn sheep, eagles, small mammals

As tough as this hike is, it continues to be one of the most popular hikes in all the Tetons. There are good reasons for this. One is that, despite the tough hike, there is a magnificent payoff at the top. When you scramble those last few yards, you are treated to a view of all the big peaks in the mountain range. Up here your head is truly in and above the clouds. This hike is also popular because it can give novices a real sense of accomplishment. Children can tell their friends they climbed a mountain.

The trail can be very busy during the month of July,

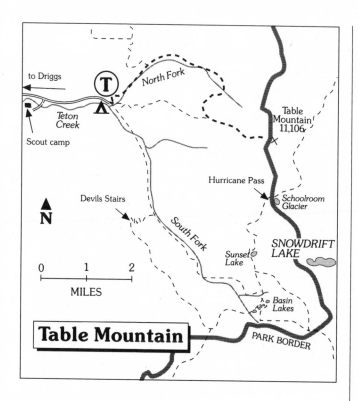

to Driggs

Teton Creek

Scout camp

North Fork

Table Mountain 11,106

Hurricane Pass

Schoolroom Glacier

N

Devils Stairs

South Fork

Sunset Lake

SNOWDRIFT LAKE

0   1   2

MILES

Basin Lakes

Table Mountain

PARK BORDER

when area Boy Scout and girls' summer camps send groups up the mountain almost daily .

The hike starts out with switchbacks for the first .5-mile, until you climb about four hundred feet. After this first initial workout, the trail settles in for a gradual incline following the North Fork of Teton Creek.

After a few hundred yards the trail enters the Jedediah Smith Wilderness Area. The wilderness designation offers this area special protections not afforded regular national forest land. The most obvious differences are that roads, mechanized vehicles, and mining are prohibited. The Forest Service has also limited the maximum number of people in each group on the trails to twenty. Groups larger than twenty must split into parties of less than twenty and remain a

Young hikers eat lunch atop Table Mountain, with fantastic views of the Grand Teton and other peaks in the background.

minimum of .5-mile apart. Certain sensitive areas, such as alpine lakes, also have special restrictive camping regulations. Consult the Jedediah Smith and Winegar Hole Wilderness map for more details on particular areas.

Wildflowers are out in abundance in the open areas along the trail during mid-July to early August. Look for moose in the willow brush near the creek.

The trail crosses the creek three times before it begins to climb more abruptly again. At about the 3.5-mile mark, the trail begins to switchback up to a high ridge. This ridge is at the 9,900-foot level. As you climb to this ridge, the trail enters into the alpine tundra zone. Here, summer is very short and few trees survive. Those that are alive are stunted, bent, and twisted. You often encounter snowfields across the trail.

All-Day and Overnight Hikes

Once you are at the top of the ridge, the thin air and lack of barriers to sight play tricks on your perception. It looks like Table Mountain is just up ahead, but in fact you've still got two miles to go and more than one thousand feet of elevation gain. From this vantage point, look for elusive bighorn sheep around the neighboring ridges and gullies.

The last mile can be very tough on tired children. Parents, be patient and let them rest often. You may have to use all your wiles to keep them going, including carrying them. Amazing as it may seem, hundreds of children hike to the top every summer.

The last hundred yards is a scramble up to the box-shaped summit, and then comes the wonderful reward. The view is breathtaking—and not just because you're out of breath. Remember to pack a camera or binoculars, because from this vantage point there is so much to see. It's also a good place to linger and eat your lunch. The flat-topped mountain summit is about as long and wide as a couple of school buses set next to each other. With a pair of binoculars we could see climbers picking their way to the top of Grand Teton.

Final Thoughts

Don't forget to bring along a pocketful of candy for yourself and the kids. It's also important to come prepared for chilly, breezy weather at the top of the mountain. The temperature can be as much as twenty degrees cooler or more at the top than on the valley floor. Should you reach the ridge at 9,900 feet and find the mountain and trail to be completely snow-covered, bag it. Turn around and call it a hike. Some snow is to be expected, but any snow makes for dangerous travel. Lastly, don't skimp on the drinking water.

Kid Comments

How can there be so much snow up here in the middle of July?

I can see for a hundred miles.

It seems like you can just reach out and touch the Grand Teton!

Tips on Hiking With Kids

Motivating children to have fun doing hard things is not an exact science. Each child responds to his or her own set of enticements and encouragements. And what works today may have the opposite effect tomorrow. Children are always changing. They change with age, the weather, their clothes, what they ate for breakfast, what's playing on the radio—you name it, and the challenge for parents is to keep in touch. Learn to know when to be firm and when to let up. Although I am no child psychologist, I do have a few tips and suggestions for introducing children to recreational hiking so that they will keep coming back for more.

If your long-term goal is to take your children on long hikes or overnight backpacking trips, such as those found in the long hikes section of this book, it almost goes without saying that you should start out small and work your way up. It is pretty easy to kill a child's enthusiasm if that first hike is a doozie. But if you take your rookie hikers on short and sweet trips and work up to medium and then long hikes, your success will be nearly assured.

One thing I like to do is informally outline the whole hike to everyone involved. I take out the map and show my family where we are, and I follow the trail with my finger. If there are interesting features on the hike, I point out on the map where we should encounter them. This routine serves the purpose of making it everyone's hike. My children may have some good suggestions for what they'd like to do on the hike, such as, "Let's eat our lunch at that lake," or "I'd like to take a picture of that waterfall." This routine eventually teaches parent and child alike how to judge a trail from the map.

Preparation is the key to success in hiking with children. A prehike checklist, whether it's in your mind or on paper, will help assure that nothing essential is left behind. Children should get plenty of rest the night before a hike. It helps to give children a list of items they can put in their packs. Be careful not to let them pack extras, or they will soon be complaining of a heavy pack and lagging behind. Once, our seven-year-old packed all her favorite books for a hike. When she was falling far behind we hefted her pack and found it to be heavier than her older sister's. Dad ended up carrying the extra weight of Dr. Suess and Sweet Pickles.

Another very important preparation is physical. You can judge a child's readiness for the trail by taking walks in your home neighborhood. If your child tires out after a block or two, then you've both got conditioning work to do. Consider the other physical activities your child does, such as walking to school, bicycle-riding, delivering newspapers, or playing soccer when evaluating fitness levels.

As you hike, praise your children for every switchback, creek crossing, or tough spot they negotiate. Take plenty of rest stops and snack breaks. It can be a tremendous psychological boost to surprise your children every once in a while with candy at the flimsiest excuse. And if you must abandon your hike because the children can't make it, take care not to place blame. Instead, try to put a positive face on the situation with comments like, "Well, we made it to the wildflowers, and that was what we wanted to see most of all," or "This is a good spot to turn around—just think of all the things we've seen!"

Ages and Abilities

It helps tremendously to match the trail to the child. The following are some generalities for linking age and abilities:

Infants. When your baby is sitting up, at about five to six months, he or she should do well in a carrier on your back. The ground you cover will depend on your physical ability.

Most child carriers reach their weight limit at about forty to forty-five pounds. This means that you can carry your child well past age three—if your back holds out. When you can no longer stuff your child into the carrier, or your little buddy weighs more than a sack of potatoes, you can sell it. Well-built child carriers usually hold their value well.

Find a carrier that has lots of padding, and a waist belt to distribute the weight to your hips. Get one that lets your baby ride high enough to see over your shoulders. The carrier should also be adjustable to accommodate the rapid growth babies go through.

Make sure your baby gets plenty to drink in hot weather. Hats or attached umbrellas are good for keeping the sun off. In cooler weather, a baby should dress a bit warmer than you because he or she will just be sitting. Be careful about achieving high altitudes (more than eight thousand feet) quickly; small children can sometimes have difficulties adjusting. Also, let junior out to run or crawl around occasionally to get the circulation going.

Toddlers and preschoolers. This is often the toughest age group to take hiking. Patience and lower expectations as far as distance is concerned will be very helpful to parents. Trails in good condition are a big help to little feet, so unless your kids are in superb condition, avoid trails with big climbs of more than six hundred feet up or down. Take lots of rest stops, and take time to look, listen, smell, and touch things—flowers, rocks, squirrels, bugs, animal tracks, songbirds—all these things help keep youngsters with short attention spans interested. The idea is to introduce youngsters gradually to the activity of hiking so that in the future they'll be excited about long hikes. It helps to think about the things kids love to do—like throwing rocks in a pond or floating stick boats in a stream or watching rodents, hawks, or bugs. Point to landmarks up ahead and say, "When we reach that point, we'll have a party." When the landmark arrives, pull out candy and water, sing a song, play a game, read a story, play with a toy, and snap a few photos.

Three- and four-year-olds can carry a small knapsack with a favorite toy or sweater and a snack. Increase the weight as the child gets older with items that the whole gang needs, such as bug repellent or lunch components.

Young children (ages 5 to 7). At this age, children should be able to make a day of it if they are in good shape. But remember to start out small and work up to longer, tougher hikes: good trails and limited elevation gains are still the best bet. Limit day hikes to about five miles.

Attention spans at these ages will last a couple of hours. When interest begins to flag, do something different for a while, like swimming, fishing, or playing games. Keeping notes of animal tracks, or counting birds or other animals can be fun at these ages. My children enjoyed singing silly songs or making up poems. You can allow some freedom and independence in hiking, but set the limits you feel comfortable with.

Often, allowing a smaller child to be trail leader for a while can do wonders for his or her speed. The thrill of being first can make all the difference. It also can force a more reasonable pace on the rest of the group. If you can arrange it, bringing along a friend of the same age and ability will work magic. The children will then slip into their own play world and often skip merrily down the trail. Expect to move along at about 1 to 1.5 miles per hour.

Older children and preadolescents (ages 8 to 12). This is a fun age group to take hiking. I am amazed at the ability of my nine-year-old to help Dad check out the occasional tough trail. If you help your children work up to it, ten miles or more a day is within reach of this age group. At these ages, children can picture in their minds a day of hiking and what lies ahead. They can also begin to carry heavier packs. Take care to limit pack weight to less than twenty-five percent of overall body weight, though. On hot days, remember to carry plenty of water. Water helps the body to reenergize itself. Without it, children (and adults) will find themselves pooping out sooner than they should. There is also the risk of heat exhaustion without plenty of water.

Make sure that children of these ages have help over tricky spots, such as narrow bridges, snowy trails, or rocky places that require some balance. A sense of balance will not be fully developed until the teen years. This age group can move along at 1.5 to 2 miles per hour, depending on the terrain.

Teens (ages 13 to 18). At this age, the young person will often walk faster than an adult and can carry nearly as much. But remember to keep pack weights at about twenty-five percent or less of the total body weight. At certain times, teenagers will experience growth spurts that can sap energy and slow them down. And with the onset of puberty, teens begin to sweat more. Make sure that plenty of water is consumed, especially on hot days or uphill hikes. Also, bring along plenty of food. Teens seem to need tons of calories to keep them going.

Teens that are in shape and used to hiking usually love a challenge. Tougher hikes to the tops of ridges, to high alpine basins, or to the deep backcountry are within reach for this age group. Overnight or longer hikes are also a good bet for experienced hikers.

Games and Activities

Many children can keep themselves amused for a long time. This is very helpful if mom and dad are fixing lunch or just need to relax for a while or you find yourself in camp with no marshmallows. Often, all it takes to keep a child occupied is a favorite toy or a book. Make sure teddy rides along if it makes your child happier. Balls, fris-

Pelicans are very large waterbirds with great throat pouches. They visit the mountain lakes during the warm months to dine on trout. From a distance they can be mistaken for swans.

bees, coloring or activity books, pails-and-shovels, kites, fishing gear, walkie-talkies, novels, and board games are all great to bring along if they are not too heavy. (I'm not a big fan of portable stereos.)

A taste of nature study can be a great children's activity. Small books that help identify flowers, insects, or animal tracks can pique a child's interest on a hike. At the discovery of a new footprint, let the child try to figure out what animal made it. Watch and listen for birds, and see if you can imitate their songs. Give children a notebook in which to sketch drawings of the animals they see or the plants and flowers that impress them. Help them learn the names of things. Make up your own names for mountains, creeks, lakes, trees, flowers, and animals, then compare your names with the real ones on the map and in your identification books.

When nature study wears thin ("Dad, I don't care *who* made that footprint!"), then it's time to turn to the old tried and true forms of entertainment. The following is a list of a few simple games and activities to help young and old make the outdoors just plain fun. Often, families have games they love to play that can be adapted for trail use.

Thicket. This is an old favorite with our family. It's a variation on hide-and-seek, so most kids pick it up almost immediately. As the names implies, terrain with trees, brush, and rocks are necessary. One child, the person who is "It," stands with eyes closed and counts to fifty. The rest of the family must hide. The main rule is that you can only hide where you can clearly see the person who is It. This automatically limits the distance you can go. After counting, the person who is It is only allowed to move one foot in an effort to spot the hiders. As people are spotted, the person who is It must correctly call out their name and position: "I see Joey behind that bush." Usually the first person caught is the next one to be It.

Blindfold. This is a simple game that works well with younger children. A child is blindfolded, and an array of items are brought before him or her to touch, smell, hear, and, if appropriate, taste. Outdoor items such as rocks, pinecones, flower petals, feathers, leaves, and so on, are best because these help children become more familiar with nature. As the child makes a guess, set the item down and go on to the next. After, say, five or six items are guessed at, the blindfold is removed for the child to see how well she or he did. To make the game more fun, you can add a reward, such as a piece of candy, for guessing a certain number of items.

Tiny worlds. This activity requires one or two pieces of equipment. First, you need a magnifying glass at least three inches in diameter. The bigger the better. For many children, a magnifying glass will provide hours of fascination. Give your children common things found along the trail, such as leaves, pinecones, or bugs, and have them examine them with the magnifying glass and tell you something about the items they never noticed without the magnifying glass. Other activities might include laying a circle of string on the ground and having children explore everything within it, using the glass. Have children count the bugs and the different kinds of leaves, follow the tiny trails, and look for things that are alive and things that are dead.

Storytelling. We've played this game in different ways. The most popular is to have one person start off a story, and after thirty seconds or so hand off the story to the person to the left. Sometimes each person will try to get the hero into as big a jam as possible for the next person to get him or her out of. Another storytelling game is "Catch the Liar." One person tells three short stories, and the rest must guess which are true and which are not.

Flashlight hike. This is a fun activity because it is so different. Each child should have his or her own flashlight to carry. On a fair-weather evening, pick out an easy trail. If you want to spot nocturnal animals, it helps if everyone speaks in hushed tones as they walk. When an animal is spotted, flash the light at its head so that everyone can see its glowing eyes. In the Tetons, night is a good time to spot beaver, mice, deer, elk, and small animals.

So You Want to Go Backpacking

During the 1970s, backpacking reached an all-time high in popularity. Yellowstone and Grand Teton national parks issued tens of thousands of backcountry permits for overnight and longer stays. Most of the users were from the Baby Boom generation. During the 1980s, the number of backcountry users fell off to about half of the peak numbers. The Baby Boomers were getting jobs, having families, and finding other adventures. But today those people who once roamed the backcountry as teens and college students are returning with their own children to introduce an old love to their offspring. If your family is experienced with car camping and day hiking, backpacking is the next logical step. All you need is a good backpack and the lighter-weight versions of most of the gear you are now using to car- camp.

If it's been more than a few years since you've gone backpacking—that is, overnight camping into the backcountry—then you will be doing yourself a great favor by checking into some of the new innovations in backpacking equipment. Like many sports, backpacking has benefitted immensely from applications of new technology. Strong, light-weight materials and new wonder fabrics have helped make recreation much easier and more enjoyable.

First, a few tips and recommendations. If your equipment is left over from your Boy Scout days or was purchased back when the Beatles were still together, then it's time to see what's new at the sporting goods store. If you are already an experienced day hiker, you'll require only a few extra pieces of equipment in order to have an enjoyable overnight trip. Parents taking children along will want to be in good physical shape because they will be carrying more than their share of the

Bald eagles patrol the ground looking for rodents, and the lakes and streams for fish. Unlike ospreys, which plunge feet first into the water to catch fish, bald eagles try to snatch their fish with their talons as they swoop over the surface of the water.

weight. This usually limits the distance they can travel. Most of the suggested backpacking trips in this book take this into consideration: most are good overnight trips for families who are experienced day hikers.

You and your family will need backpacks. At first glance, most backpacks look a lot alike. But as with most things in life, there are cheap imitations of the real thing in abundance. I don't mean to promote brand-name snobbery, but my suggestion is to go with an established company with a reputation for quality.

Today's backpacks fall into two main categories: external-frame packs and internal-frame packs. External-frame packs are great for carrying heavy loads and for trail hiking. Internals tend to carry loads with a lower center of gravity, making them good for off-trail hiking, Nordic skiing, and mountain climbing. Externals are less touchy when it comes to loading gear; internals are more picky about what goes where. Internals are often very comfortable, especially for women, but the latest external packs have come a long way in comfort. Because internal-frame packs hug your back, they can be much hotter, a concern in the summertime. Externals give your back a little more breathing room.

For novice backpackers, I think the safest bet is to go with an external-frame pack at first. Be aware that few packs fit children younger than eleven years old. To compensate for this, look for some of the smaller rucksacks or internal-frame packs that feature a padded waist belt, or check into some of the downsized frame packs made by Kelty, Camp Trails, and Peak 1. Be careful about getting a very large pack for children: they shouldn't be carrying more than twenty-five percent of their weight. Adults should start out carrying about twenty percent of their weight and then work up to about thirty percent.

For adults, look for a thick, comfortable waist belt and shoulder straps that easily adjust to height and chest size. Sternum straps are very helpful. Try on packs in the store and have the salesperson add weights. Walk around for a while, then try on another pack and do some comparing. The pack, if properly fitted, should place about seventy-five percent of its weight on your hips. If it doesn't, try a different pack. I am continually amazed to see backpackers on the trail using packs with no waist belts at all. My feeling is that any load weighing more than fifteen pounds should be in a pack with a waist belt.

If you find a store that rents gear, try an internal-frame pack one week and an external-frame pack the next to see which one suits you best. If the store rents different brands, take time to try out the ones you like.

The next most important piece of equipment is a sleeping bag. A sleepless night of shivering in the backcountry will kill a family's enthusiasm for backpacking quickly. But those huge, bulky bags that are used for car camping are too heavy and too hard to stuff into a pack. It isn't necessary, though, to buy one of those costly lightweight down bags. Fortunately, recent innovations in synthetic materials have made sleeping bags cheaper, lighter in weight, and less bulky.

There are two things I look for first: the overall weight of the bag, and warmth. To be suited for backpacking, a sleeping bag should weigh less than four pounds—the lighter the better. I look for bags in the three-pound or less range. Unless you can afford down sleeping bags, which offer the best weight-to-warmth ratio, the issue becomes a trade-off of weight to warmth. But if you are planning on using the bag for mostly summer backpacking (which is what most of us do), then look for bags in the three-pound range that will keep you warm to about twenty to thirty degrees. In the Tetons, summertime lows average around forty degrees. A thirty-degree bag should do just fine, especially if you use a tent. The mummy-bag style is usually the warmest.

Look for materials that hold up well. I don't buy down bags for children because down bags require special handling and cleaning. Kid bags usually need to be cleaned more often, and definitely take more abuse. If you are bringing along a toddler or a baby on an overnight trip, a zipped-up down coat makes a fine sleeping bag.

Adults should consider using an air mattress. This can make the difference between a good night's rest and a night of misery. Children are much more flexible and can get by with lightweight, inexpensive Ensolite pads.

After the pack and sleeping bags, getting a packstove should be next on your list. It is possible to go without a stove by using a campfire or by packing foods that don't require cooking. But I prefer a stove because some areas, especially national parks or designated wilderness areas, forbid campfires. I also like the flexibility that a pack stove offers in allowing me to make a variety of meals.

If you are used to using a camp stove when car camping, I suggest that you try the same style of stove in the one-burner lightweight pack size. There are several brands, styles, and philosophies in pack stoves. Once again, quality and ease of use count the most. Pack stoves can often be rented from sporting goods stores, which gives you a chance to test some.

Get to know your pack stove inside and out before you take your first trip. A quality stove should give years of service. Many backpackers, myself included, often talk about their pack stoves as if they were dear friends. Find the right one and you will, too.

Along with a stove, you'll need some cooking utensils. My cooking gear comes from the second-hand store. You can buy complete a cooking set at a sporting goods store, but you probably won't need all the pots, pans, cups, and whatnots that come with it. For our family's style of cooking, we find a two-quart aluminum coffeepot and a one-and-a-half-quart saucepan is all we need. Both pots have lids. The coffeepot boils water for hot cocoa and freeze-dried meals, and the saucepan is for "fancier" meals like oatmeal or macaroni and cheese. If we are planning on eating trout, we either poach the fish in the saucepan or bring along some aluminum foil and "bake" the wrapped fish over campfire coals. Each person carries a spoon, a heavy-duty plastic cup, and a lightweight plastic bowl. That's it. Any more than this to us is just extra weight.

Backpackers will need a way to purify water. Water in the Tetons, or anywhere in the Rocky Mountains, for that matter, is just not safe to drink without first being purified. Day hikers can get by taking along an extra bottle of water, but backpackers can't afford the extra weight.

There are three ways to purify water: boil it, filter it, or "poison" it. The lightest-weight method is to drop iodine tablets into the water. This has its drawbacks: it gives the water a yucky taste, according to my kids, and it can also cause medical problems for some people over time. Boiling water is the tried-and-true method, but it also has drawbacks. You have to pack along extra fuel for the pack stove, which means extra weight, and it takes time to boil ice-cold mountain stream water. The third method, using a filter, is becoming the most popular. A filter removes all the bugs and gunk and pumps clean water into your bottle or cooking pot. The nice thing about filters is that they are almost immediate. You can drink ice-cold water from the stream any time you want, after a little pumping. On long day hikes that follow streams or lakes, pack a small bottle and your filter instead of a couple of large full bottles. (Children enjoy water duty while camping.) The down side is that a quality filter system costs thirty-five dollars and up.

Kids love tents. Good backpacking tents that weigh less than eight pounds and that will sleep a family of four will cost some money. But a good tent can make a big difference on many overnighters. It will give you a place to duck into during those sudden thundershowers that come and go in the Tetons. It will also keep out the mosquitoes and other bugs that drive children and parents crazy.

Families should look for tents with enough headroom to allow adults to sit up inside. Look into tents that are easy to set up and that will hold up well in wind and rain. Check for overall quality, tough materials, and well-made reinforcements. A tent is another item you may want to rent, if possible, before purchase.

If you don't have a tent, don't let that stop you from backpacking. With some careful planning, you can do without. Follow the weather reports, which are usually accurate in the Tetons, and go later in the summer, when there are fewer mosquitoes. Use a plastic tarp to sleep on. You can help children pick out constellations while lying under the stars and thus enhance the experience.

Grand Teton National Park
Rules for Backcountry Use

• Overnight campers in the backcountry must obtain the required non-fee backcountry permit at the Moose or Colter Bay visitor centers, or the Jenny Lake Ranger Station.

- Although berry picking is allowed in the park, it is important not to overdo it. Remember that berries are an important source of food for some animals.
- Pack stoves are required for cooking. Due to the scarcity of wood and related ecological hazards in the high country, wood or charcoal fires are prohibited.
- Urinate at least 150 feet from streams and lakes. To prevent contamination of waterways, bury feces in a hole six to eight inches deep and at least 150 feet from streams and lakes. Pack out used toilet paper or carefully burn it, provided fire danger is low. Store used tampons, sanitary napkins, and diapers in sealed plastic bags and pack them out. Do not bury or burn them.
- Camp out of sight of trails and other campers. In trailed canyons, camp on previously used campsites.
- Camp at least one hundred feet from lakes and streams.
- Advance reservations are required for group campsites in the backcountry.
- Hike on established trails to prevent erosion. Don't shortcut trails.
- Horse parties have the right-of-way on trails. Step off the trail and remain quiet as horses pass.
- When photographing wildlife, keep a safe distance. Do not feed or approach wildlife.
- Keep stock animals out of camping areas. Use hitch rails where provided. Do not tie stock to live trees.
- To prevent polluting streams and lakes, don't wash dishes or bathe in the water.
- Carry out all trash.
- Pets, motorized equipment, wheeled vehicles, bicycles, firearms, and fireworks are prohibited in the backcountry.

Elk, or wapiti, can be distinguished from deer by their size and color. Elk stand about 5 feet at the shoulder, have dark brown legs, a pale brown yellowish rump, and a short tail. Males have a shaggy neck mane. They are usually seen in groups of twenty or more.

Other Activities

Biking

There are several nice bicycle trips around the Tetons for those who bring along their bikes or plan to rent one during their stay.

I do not recommend family bicycle travel on the highways in and around the Tetons. Many of the routes have wide shoulders suitable for touring bikes, but the intense traffic can make them dangerous. For touring bikes, I recommend the bike path along the one-way road from Jenny Lake to String Lake, and the paved road across Antelope Flats.

If you are riding fat-tire bikes or mountain bikes, you have more options. One of the best routes in the park for mountain bikers is the Snake River Road. This dirt road is your first left past the Signal Mountain Road as you drive south from the Signal Mountain Lodge. The bumpy dirt road goes for about fourteen miles and features the Tetons on one side and the Snake River on the other. Another, tougher, route into the Tetons is up Phillips Canyon. Because this is national forest land, bikes are allowed on the trails to Ski Lake and along much of Phillips Canyon. Two other nice routes suitable for family mountan biking include the Ditch Creek Road on the east side of the park north of the Gros Ventre River, and the Shadow Mountain loop road just north of Ditch Creek Road.

Another popular route for mountain bikers is along the Game Creek Trail to the Cache Creek Trail. These trails are near Jackson and travel through heavily wooded backcountry. They are easy to moderate in difficulty. To get to Cache Creek from Jackson, go to

Redmond Street in East Jackson and turn onto Cache Creek Drive. You can ride up the dirt road until you reach the Gros Ventre Wilderness boundaries, or turn up a steep trail that connects into Game Creek. The Game Creek Trail ends at Highway 89.

The Bridger-Teton National Forest Buffalo and Jackson Ranger District Map has all the above-mentioned trips on it. Bike shops are also a good reference for other, more challenging trails.

When riding mountain bikes on backcountry trails, keep in mind a few rules. Bikes are not allowed on any trails in designated wilderness areas, nor are they allowed on the hiking trails in the national parks. If you do take to some of the backcountry trails on national forest land, practice good trail etiquette. Bicyclists should give hikers and horseback riders the right-of-way. A mountain bike zipping down the trail can be an alarming sight for skittish horses or hikers absorbed in the scenery. It's also a good idea to outfit your family with helmets and gloves. Don't forget to fill your water bottles before you take off.

Canoeing

Hiking is not the only exciting family activity going on in the Tetons. If you bring along your canoe, or rent a canoe on your visit to the area, you can test the waters of several lakes and streams. Some trails are best checked out in combination with a canoe ride.

There are several nice things about a canoe. It can get you to some backcountry campsites that otherwise would be very tough for a family to hike to. Anglers can also more readily find the fish in the smaller lakes with a canoe. And a canoe trip can be a welcome respite for young legs recuperating from the previous day's hiking.

If you are planning a canoe trip inside the park, you will need a boating permit. These can be picked up at any of the park's visitor centers. Rental canoes from Jackson or inside the park will already have a boating permit on them.

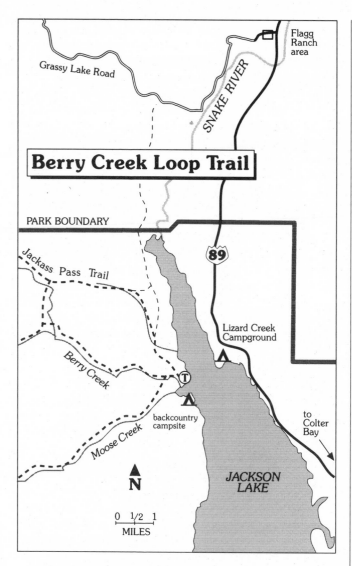

Berry Creek Loop Trail

Flagg Ranch area

Grassy Lake Road

SNAKE RIVER

PARK BOUNDARY

Jackass Pass Trail

89

Berry Creek

Lizard Creek Campground

Moose Creek

T

backcountry campsite

to Colter Bay

N

0 1/2 1
MILES

JACKSON LAKE

Family canoeing places in Jackson Hole are limited to six lakes and the Snake River. The lakes include Jenny, String, Leigh, Jackson, and Two Ocean in the national park. Outside of the park there is Lower Slide Lake. The Snake River around Oxbow Bend also offers nice canoeing. Phelps, Emma Matilda, Taggart, Bradley, and Bearpaw lakes also allow hand-propelled vessels, but hauling a canoe cross-country to reach these lakes would be arduous at best for most families.

The wind can make canoeing a major chore on some of the lakes. Storms on some of the larger lakes can come up quickly and make canoeing dangerous. Paying attention to the weather forecasts and possible afternoon thunderstorms is important.

Here is a quick review of the seven canoeing areas mentioned above:

Jenny Lake: At first glance, Jenny Lake may not seem all that big. Yet it is more than 1 mile wide and about 1.5 miles long. Access to the water is via a boat ramp .5-mile west of the Jenny Lake east boat dock, not far from the visitor center. You can put together a nice canoe-hiking trip by paddling across to the west boat dock (be sure to keep out of the way of the shuttle boat) and then hiking up to Hidden Falls and Inspiration Point. Anglers will want to troll for trout and check out the inlets on the northwest side.

String Lake: This narrow, small lake lies between Jenny and Leigh lakes. To reach its waters, drive toward the String Lake picnic area. Before you get to the picnic area, there is a nice area for launching a canoe. This shallow water is also great for swimming on a hot day.

Leigh Lake: This lake requires a portage from String Lake. With a light enough canoe and help from all hands, the short hike, .15-mile, is not too bad. This lake offers some of the best sandy-beach campsites in the area. There are two sites on the east side of the south arm and three more on the far west side, near the inlets from Paintbrush Canyon and Leigh Canyon. There is also a group campsite near the east-side beach about two miles from String Lake. The easy paddle across Leigh Lake is perfect for a secluded picnic or overnight campout. There are also some nice unmaintained trails on the west side of the lake and up the two west-side canyons.

Jackson Lake: There are two fun areas I recommend for canoeing in this monster lake. The first is right around Colter Bay: there are many points and inlets just south of Colter Bay that can take most of the day to explore. If you want an overnight adventure, there is a campsite on the point that separates Colter Bay from Little Mackinaw Bay, and a much more distant campsite on the southeast side of Hermitage Point.

Farther north, where Jackson Lake narrows, you can paddle across from Lizard Creek Campground to Wilcox Point. There is a campsite at Wilcox Point. Two creeks, Moose Creek and Owl Creek, enter the lake in a small bay next to Wilcox Point. This is prime habitat for waterfowl, beaver, moose, and eagles. On the opposite side of this bay is a trailhead. To find the trail, look for a tall post that is painted white at the top. This trail leads into a series of routes leading up Webb Canyon, Owl Creek Canyon, and Berry Creek Canyon. There is an easy 3.2-mile trail up Lower Berry Creek through a narrow canyon to the junction with Owl Creek. You can make this a loop hike by continuing up Berry Creek and clockwise around Elk Ridge and returning back to the trailhead. This route is about 7.75 miles of mostly easy walking. These trails receive few visitors compared to the crowds that flock to the central Teton canyons. Many elk bands summer in this area and occasional groups of bighorn sheep can be seen along the canyons.

Two Ocean Lake: This is often a good lake to paddle when winds are plaguing the other lakes along the Tetons. The road to Two Ocean Lake is about a mile north of Moran Junction. The lake is about three miles long and a haven for waterfowl, beavers, bears, deer, elk, and moose. Probably the best way to fish this lake is from a canoe. Swimming is not recommended because of cold-water leeches and poor water quality. Maintaining silence will help you spot some wildlife along the shore as you cruise around the lake.

A pair of canoeists paddles along String Lake.

Oxbow Bend. This is a popular section of the Snake River, where large meanders form quiet backwater. Oxbow Bend is a mile east of the Jackson Lake junction. There are plenty of slack-water areas above and below the Cattleman's Bridge to give paddlers a rest from the river currents. This is a good place to see waterfowl: geese, swans, ducks, and pelicans are often seen at fairly close range throughout the bend. Moose and other big game often pass through this area. Fishing is also popular here. Canoes should not stray any farther downstream from the Oxbow Bend area: past the slack area is faster and rougher water that is unsuitable for family canoeing.

Slide Lake. This lake is just outside the park, about 5.5 miles east of Kelly. Slide Lake was formed by a gigantic landslide in 1925 that blocked the Gros Ventre River. The lake is about 2.5 miles long and about .5-mile wide. As you paddle around the lake you will see the remains of old tree stands sticking up through the surface of the water. The leafless, lifeless trees are eerie to see from the canoe.

Fishing can be good at times on the lake. Trophy-sized lake trout inhabit these waters, but trollers must beware of the occasional snags from submerged trees.

The wind can at times be troublesome on this lake. Try early-morning or late-evening hours to avoid some of the breezes. There is a Forest Service campground with a boat launch on a point midway along the lake. You can spend the night here or just use the boat launch.

Cross-Country Skiing and Showshoeing

If you come to the Tetons in the wintertime, be prepared for some magic. Visiting the wilderness under a blanket of snow is an unforgettable experience. Cross-country, or Nordic, skiing equipment is inexpensive to rent and easy to learn how to use. Most people, including children, get the hang of it after a few hours on the trail.

The national park has a few trails flagged for cross-country skiing during the winter. These include the trail up to Phelps Lake Overlook, the Taggart Lake to Beaver Creek trails, Taggart Lake to Jenny Lake, Swan Lake and Heron Pond, and the Flagg Ranch trail along the Snake River. There are other areas in the park that may not be flagged but that are also good skiing trails. Check in at the Moose Visitor Center for recommendations for other areas suitable for your family's abilities.

Trails outside the park that are good for Nordic skiing include the Ski Lake, Huckleberry Hot Springs, and Gros Ventre Slide trails, as well as the unplowed road up Teton Creek toward the Alaska Basin trailhead.

The park conducts ranger-led snowshoe trips along the Snake River near Moose. These trips usually last a few hours and are held several times a week. Check at the Moose Visitor Center for a schedule of winter activities.

Horseback Riding

Taking a horseback ride in the mountains can be an exciting addition to your visit in the Tetons. There are several places to rent horses in the Teton area. Prices vary and often depend on whether or not lunches or other extras are included. It's a good idea to make a few phone calls using the Jackson, Wyoming, yellow pages to get an idea of what is available and what best suits your family.

Trail rides are offered by the hour in some areas, such as at Colter Bay and Jackson Lake Lodge, and there are half-day and all-day rides and even overnight or longer rides available. The rides go deep into the Tetons or just around the ranch, depending on the outfit you choose to rent from.

Index